Stavros Pechlivanidis

Companies and Virtual 3D Worlds

Stavros Pechlivanidis

Companies and Virtual 3D Worlds

Analysis of Business Models at the Example of
Second Life

VDM Verlag Dr. Müller

Imprint

Bibliographic information by the German National Library: The German National Library lists this publication at the German National Bibliography; detailed bibliographic information is available on the Internet at http://dnb.d-nb.de.

Cover image: www.purestockx.com

Publisher:
VDM Verlag Dr. Müller Aktiengesellschaft & Co. KG, Dudweiler Landstr. 125 a, 66123 Saarbrücken, Germany,
Phone +49 681 9100-698, Fax +49 681 9100-988,
Email: info@vdm-verlag.de

Produced in USA and UK by:
Lightning Source Inc., La Vergne, Tennessee, USA
Lightning Source UK Ltd., Milton Keynes, UK
BookSurge LLC, 5341 Dorchester Road, Suite 16, North Charleston, SC 29418, USA

ISBN: 978-3-639-01839-4

I dedicate this work to my father

Acknowledgments

Working now for over six years as IT consultant, the new hype about virtual 3D worlds, the 3D Internet, MMORPG's and the promise of unpreceeded business opportunities, was a subject of much interest to me. As one of my pasttimes is gaming in all flavors, I decided to take this opportunity and look into this subject from an economic and consulting perspective in the course of my MBA studies. This master thesis is the result of my research and thoughts together with uncountable input from many friends, colleagues and virtual world residents.

At this point I would like to thank especialy the people, who supported and helped me during the research for and development of this master thesis; they are, in alphabetical order:

Manfred Bundschuh, Pete Ellis, Thomas Freisberg, John P. Harding, Fang-ting Kuo-Pechlivanidis, Mahmoud Muscati, Peter Thomas, Christoph Wamser, all *interview partners* and the *Arc role-playing group* for the heated but enjoyable discussions on the subject.

Finally I also want to thank my parents for the love and kindness in our home, which made me the person I am today.

April 2008, Bonn   Stavros Pechlivanidis

Contents

List of Figures

List of Tables

Acronyms

2D Two-dimensional

3D Three-dimensional

ACM Association for Computing Machinery

ACS Anshe Chung Studios

ARPANET Advanced Research Projects Agency Network

ATM Automated Teller Machine

AW Active Worlds

B2B Business to Business

B2C Business to Consumer

C2B Consumer to Business

C2C Consumer to Consumer

ESA Entertainment Software Association

EU Entropia Universe

EULA End User License Agreement

FAQ Frequently Asked Questions

GOM Gaming Open Market

HTML HyperText Markup Language

IGDA International Game Developers Association

IGE Internet Gaming Entertainment

IDSA Interactive Digital Software Association

IP Intellectual Property

ISP Internet Service Provider

LL Linden Lab

MMO Massively Multiplayer Online game

MMORPG Massively Multiplayer Online Role-Playing Game

NPC Non Player Character

PEST Political, Economic, Social, and Technological

RPG Role-Playing Game

SL Second Life

SOE Sony Online Entertainment Inc.

TOS Terms of Service

URL Uniform Resource Locator

VR Virtual Reality

VRML Virtual Reality Modeling Language

WoW World of Warcraft

WWW World Wide Web

Chapter 1

Introduction

Today one can observe a huge rise in the hype around something called *Second Life*[1]. In February 2007, *Welt am Sonntag* dedicated three pages to Second Life in its culture section. *Der Spiegel*, the biggest news magazine in Germany, made Second Life the cover story with a 13 page report concentrating on the social implications of this virtual 3D world (Casati et al. 2007). In March 2007, the economy journal *Capital* did a nine page cover story, looking at the economic implications of the *Megatrend "Second Life"* (Schneider and Schubert 2007).

It is still not clear, what Second Life really is. Is it just another *Web 2.0* application? If so this media coverage should be viewed as part of the Web 2.0 hype observed by Gartner (Phifer et al. 2006) and Saugatuck Technology (Koenig 2007). Is it just a MMORPG[2]? Then it is a waste of time for business outside the entertainment industry. Or is it something else? In this case it would be wise to analyze the phenomenon to determine what it is exactly and how it will influence current e-business.

1.1 Virtual 3D worlds as the next step of the Internet?

To determine the relevance of virtual 3D worlds the author will first look at the evolution of the Internet and the concurrent evolution of user interfaces. He will

---

[1]Many of the designations used by companies to distinguish their brands and products are claimed as trademarks. Where those designations appear in this book, and the author was aware of a trademark claim, the designations have been printed with initial capital letters or in all capitals.

[2]Massively Multiplayer Online Role-Playing Game

then show why e-business is of strategic relevance to businesses and conclude this section with a look at the future prospects of Web 2.0 and virtual 3D worlds.

The Internet and user interface evolution: Looking back in retrospect, one can observe the number of users of the Internet increase with increasing *standardization, ease of content creation* and *content accessibility*.

In 1973 ARPANET[3], the U.S. government network for military and research purposes, started. All computer networks that followed connected to ARPANET thereby building an interconnected network. With communication protocol *standardization* the networks grew at an exponential rate and transformed from interconnected networks to the *Internet* (Tanenbaum 1996, pp. 47-52). The breakthrough came with the introduction of a new application called *WWW*[4] invented by Tim Berners-Lee in 1989 (Jacobs 2007).

With the growth rate described by Zakon (2006), the plain command line user interface, which was state of the art in the 70ies, soon became an access barrier. With the introduction of the Mosaic[5] viewer the interface changed in March 1993 from the one-dimensional command line form used in *Email, News, Remote login* and *File transfer* applications to the graphical two-dimensional form used for the WWW application today (Jacobs 2005). This change made the Internet more *accessible* for non-technical people (Tanenbaum 1996, pp. 52-54) and the concurrent development of HTML[6] made the *content creation easier* for content providers. The research into the next step of this user interface evolution, the introduction of the third dimension, had already begun and resulted into the VRML[7] specification in 1994 (Vacca 1996, p. 40). However this approach did not take off, as *bandwidth, computing* and *graphic power* was still too low in the mid 90ies. Also VR[8] was envisioned with a data glove and a head mounted display, both being too expensive and cumbersome for the mass market. Virtual 3D worlds on the other hand, were first used for games and became a big success, as the reader will see in section 2.2 later on.

---

[3]Advanced Research Projects Agency Network
[4]World Wide Web
[5]*Mosaic* is the predecessor of today's web browsers, like *Firefox* or *Internet Explorer*.
[6]HyperText Markup Language
[7]Virtual Reality Modeling Language
[8]Virtual Reality

The strategic relevance of e-business: In October 1997 IBM introduced the term *e-business* to the business world (Nelson 2001). E-business is "In simplest terms, [...] everything you do online" (Bonnett 2000). The impact of e-business as a way to use computer networks for business and commercial purposes was huge and changed the business environment fundamentally. Wirtz classified the changes into *4-forces of e-business* (Wirtz 2001, p. 151 et sqq.):

- *Increased competition*, caused by increased market transparency, decreasing entry barriers, low switching cost and disintermediation

- *Virtualization* of products, organizations, alliances and networks

- *Increased complexity* via shorter innovation cycles and market fragmentation

- *Changes in customer behavior* toward higher buying power, decreasing customer loyalty and higher information sharing

Doppler and Lauterburg describe similar direct and indirect consequences of those shifts in speed of change, power and competition intensity (Doppler and Lauterburg 2005, pp. 22-36). Summing up it is clear that e-business is of strategic importance to company success.

Web 2.0 and virtual 3D worlds: The growth of customers into virtual communities described by Wirtz has steadily increased since 2000 (Wirtz 2001, pp. 175-180). It is the core around which Web 2.0 technology and applications evolved. The term *Web 2.0* was first coined by Dale Dougherty of O'Reilly Media in 2004 (McFedries 2006). It is described by O'Reilly (2005) and again by Subramanian (2007) with seven principles:

1. The web as platform

2. Harnessing collective intelligence

3. Data is the next *Intel inside*

4. End of the software release cycle

5. Lightweight programming models

6. Software above the level of a single device

7. Rich user experience

While characteristics 1, 4, 5 and 6 describe Web 2.0 from a software development point of view, *harnessing collective intelligence* describes Web 2.0 from a user
point of view encompassing all applications, which let users collaborate with
each other in any feasible way. From a business point of view this collaboration
means a "paradigm shift from the Web as a publishing medium to a medium of
interaction and participation" (Lassila and Hendler 2007), and therefore the need
for new business models.

The future development of Web 2.0 applications faces two major challenges. The
first challenge, referring to *data as the next Intel inside*, is to develop a scalable content organization to make *Semantic Web*, also termed *Web 3.0*, successful (Hendler
2007). The second challenge, referring to *rich user experience*, lies in an intuitive interface and tool set, as "providing friendly tools for user participation in content
creation, consumption, and distribution has been key to success (and failure)"
(Lin 2007).

Virtual 3D worlds represent a giant leap in *rich user experience*, as they "satisfy two
key aspects of being human: our innately social and visual natures" (IBM 2007a),
by increasing *content accessibility*. As closed environments, virtual 3D worlds also
represent a *standard* platform with *standard* tools, making *content creation easier*.
Though virtual 3D worlds have similarities to Web 2.0, they are more than that.

1.2   Objective of the thesis

The research purpose of this thesis is to explore business opportunities and business models used in the context of virtual 3D worlds. To accomplish this, virtual
3D worlds are first analyzed and embedded into the context of new technologies,
like Web 2.0. This analysis includes the analysis of virtual 3D worlds as products,
as well as an analysis of the macro environmental factors, market and consumer
characteristics pertaining to virtual 3D worlds. The product analysis goes deeper,
including the product life cycle, the characteristics of the different product categories and key success factors of virtual 3D worlds.

Business models derived from the virtual world value-chain are then described
using the example of Second Life, to date the most famous virtual 3D world not

intended for gaming. The characteristics of these business models are examined and evaluated to identify the threats and opportunities associated with them. In detail the following questions will be explored:

- Why are virtual 3D worlds interesting from a business perspective?
- What are the characteristics of virtual 3D worlds in general and that of Second Life in particular?
- What business models can be implemented in and around Second Life?
- What are the threats and opportunities of such an engagement?

The following subjects, although influencing the research area to some degree, are out of scope, due to the size restrictions of this thesis:

- 3D applications in production, construction and research or applications like *Google Earth*
- Thorough analysis of online gaming worlds or the gaming industry
- Comparison against Web 2.0 applications
- Technical description of virtual 3D worlds or web-based technologies
- Implementation strategies to realize the business models described

The terms *virtual 3D world* and *virtual world* will be used interchangeably for convenience.

1.3 Approach and methodology of the thesis

A single case study research strategy was pursued which focused on Second Life with embedded cases representing implementations of the identified business models.

Research was conducted using a mix of secondary and primary data. To investigate and describe the context of virtual 3D worlds and business models, documentary and survey-based secondary data were used[9]. Considering the strong relation Second Life seems to have with MMORPG worlds, Web 2.0 and cyberculture the author studied three bodies of literature: one relating to virtual 3D

---

[9]For a definition of *secondary data* types refer to Saunders et al. (2007, pp. 248-253)

worlds, Web 2.0 and Second Life in particular, another relating to studies around cyber-culture and the social implications of VR and the last concerned with business models in a changing e-business environment.

Qualitative primary data were collected in the form of semi-structured and unstructured one-to-one interviews[10] for the main part of this thesis[11]. The interview partners are consumers of virtual 3D worlds.

The master thesis is divided up into three parts. In chapter 2 the reader is introduced to the concept of the *business model* used by the author throughout the thesis and to the fundamentals of virtual 3D worlds in general as well as Second Life in particular. These fundamentals encompass the virtual 3D world value-chain, an introduction to the different virtual world types and the key success factors for virtual 3D world applications in general. They are derived from success prerequisites collected through expert interviews or secondary data.

In chapter 3 the attractiveness of the virtual 3D world industry is examined. Firstly the macro environment of virtual 3D worlds is analyzed, using the PEST[12] analysis technique described by Narayanan and Fahey[13]. Then the virtual 3D world industry is segmented along three segmentation variables using the segmentation analysis approach described by Porter[14]. The chapter concludes with the deduction of the business models particular to virtual 3D worlds, using the value-chain deconstruction and reconstruction approach described by Timmers[15]. In chapter 4 the business models identified previously will be explored further using three case studies. The segmentation analysis methodology described by Porter[16] is used to analyze and evaluate each case described. Chapter 5 concludes the thesis with a summary of the researched results.

---

[10]For readability the term *semi-structured and unstructured one-to-one interviews* will be abbreviated with *expert interviews*.

[11]For a definition of interview *types* refer to Saunders et al. (2007, pp. 312-314)

[12]Political, Economic, Social, and Technological

[13]A brief introduction to this methodology can be found in appendix A.2.

[14]A brief introduction to this methodology can be found in appendix A.3.

[15]A brief introduction to this methodology can be found in appendix A.1.

[16]A brief introduction to this methodology can be found in appendix A.3.

Chapter 2

Fundamentals

This chapter introduces the reader to the fundamentals necessary to understand the remaining chapters. In section 2.1 business models are described, while virtual worlds and the virtual world value-chain are introduced in section 2.2. Second Life, the world chosen as reference object is introduced in section 2.3.

2.1 Fundamentals on business models

The definition of business models and their purpose from a strategic perspective are described in subsection 2.1.1. In 2.1.2 general business models in an e-business context are introduced, and finally a closer look is taken at the general key success factors of e-business models in 2.1.3.

2.1.1 Character and features of business models

The term *business model* is used in different context and varying scope throughout economic literature. Osterwalder et al. analyzed the use of this term from 1990 to 2003 and developed the following definition:

> A business model is a conceptual tool that contains a set of elements and their relationships and allows expressing the business logic of a specific firm. It is a description of the value a company offers to one or several segments of customers and of the architecture of the firm and its network of partners for creating, marketing, and deliv-

ering this value and relationship capital, to generate profitable and sustainable revenue streams. (Osterwalder et al. 2005, p. 17-18)

Osterwalder et al. developed a business model concept consisting of nine related business model building blocks (see figure 2.1), that can be mapped to the general business model concept described by Wirtz (2001, p. 211, figure 76). While Wirtz gives a good definition of the term suitable for e-business, Osterwalder et al. can be regarded as more concise due to the research approach used. Either way, a complete description of such a concept/model in the following chapters of this thesis would take too much space and is therefore out of scope. Therefore the author will confine the term *business model* to the *Value Proposition* building block, giving "an overall view of a company's bundle of products and services"[1] within the context of virtual worlds, which fits perfectly into the value-chain approach to identify new business models in section 3.3.

Business models can be used to formulate and realize strategic objectives[2]. Wirtz

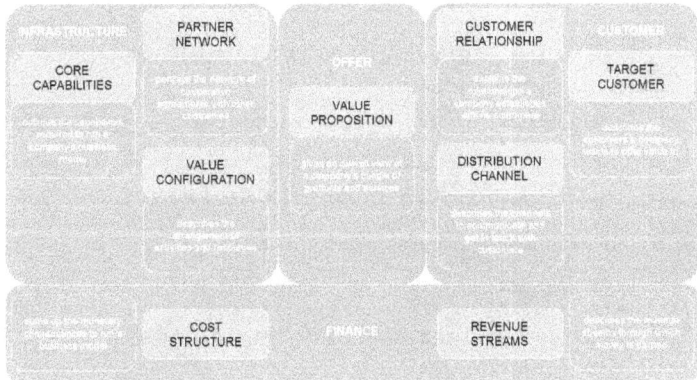

Figure 2.1: Business Model Concept according to (Osterwalder 2006)

describes four levels of strategy formulation (Wirtz 2001, pp. 183-186), whereas Grant identifies only three (Grant 2005, pp. 22-23). Wirtz added the *relation Level* as fourth level, where strategies are formulated with the objective of strengthening partner relationships. For this thesis the fourth level will be neglected, since

---

[1](see Osterwalder 2006, in `business-model-template-5677.ppt` p. 3) or figure 2.1

[2]*Formulate* strategic objectives through the *Value Proposition* business model building block and develop a strategy taking into account competition to *realize* those strategic objectives.

partner or customer relationship management is seen by the author as part of increasing effectiveness of functional strategies implemented by procurement or marketing and sales departments. Only the first three levels are therefore considered in the following discussion. At each level the associated strategic objective is different. For example, on a corporate level the objective would be to create value, whereas on a functional level within the marketing and sales function the objective would be to increase effectiveness and efficiency of the chosen marketing and sales activities. Table 2.1 shows examples of value proposition business models in the context of a specific strategy level and its associated strategic objective. Based on those value propositions the company can build its strategies by also taking into account the relevant competitors, as business models do not consider competitors (Grant 2005, pp. 15-18).

With the general definition of the term *business model* and the description of its

Strategy Level	Strategic Objective	Value Proposition Examples
Corporate level	Create value	• Designing virtual products • Organizing events • Hosting virtual worlds • Offering a trading platform
Business level	Create and sustain competitive advantage	• Expanding web design services to 3D design • Expand retail banking services to virtual worlds • Establish virtual fashion unit
Functional level	Increase effectiveness and efficiency	• Integrate virtual worlds into marketing and sales activities • Use virtual worlds for e-learning • Use virtual worlds for internal corporate communication

Table 2.1: Strategic objectives on different strategy levels

function within the strategy planning process, different forms of business models within the e-business environment can now be examined.

2.1.2   Forms of e-business models

E-business models are always distinguished along business areas based on the interaction between the *consumer*, *business* and *government* actors (Wirtz 2001, p. 35). Within the thesis context the actor *government* is not relevant, so it is omitted in further discussions. Table 2.2 describes all possible interaction permutations between *consumer* and *business* with the term *interaction* encompassing *information exchange*, *communication* and *transactions* (Kollmann 2007, p. 40).

This classification based on interaction types is criticized by Wirtz, as these cat-

Abbr.	Relation	Description
B2B	Business to Business	Interaction through electronic networks between businesses
B2C	Business to Consumer	Business interaction through electronic networks to consumers
C2B	Consumer to Business	Consumer interaction through electronic networks to businesses
C2C	Consumer to Consumer	Interactions through electronic networks between consumers

Table 2.2: Supply-demand interactions between *Business* and *Consumer* actors

egories lead to double coverage of business models and also to either too heterogeneous groups or contrary to too many categories (Wirtz 2001, pp. 217-218). He proposes a business model classification named *4C-Net-Business Model*, which is based on offered services found in the Internet. They do not fit to the virtual world context perfectly though, since virtual worlds differ from the Internet, as will be seen in section 2.2. As an example the model *Content* is confined to the *own* platform. If a business offers content within a virtual world it is content on a *provided* platform. Therefore the author used the more general interaction based classification seen in table 2.2.

2.1.3   Success factors of e-business models

Grant used the term *key success factors* within the context of strategy planning "to identify those factors within the firm's market environment that determine its ability to survive and prosper" (Grant 2005, p. 92[3]). *Key success factors* are derived from *prerequisites for success* by analyzing demand, i.e. customer needs, and competition, i.e. things needed to do by the company to survive competition (Grant 2005, p. 93).

For e-business models outside any industry or competition context key success

---

[3]Grant used the term first coined by Chuck Hofer and Dan Schendel, *Strategy Formulation: Analytical Concepts* (St. Paul: West Publishing, 1977) (Grant 2005, p. 99).

factors can only be derived from the demand side prerequisites for success. Conducting a survey among 111 leading Finnish companies, Horsti et al. identified general prerequisites of e-business model success[4] which are applicable to all e-business models, regardless of industry, company or manager (Horsti et al. 2005):

- Secured e-business for customers

- Management's commitment for the e-business development

- Easiness to use e-business products and services

- Stability of hardware and software

With regard to the reduced scope of the term *business model* defined on page 18, the question arises, as to whether the reduction affects the applicability of the prerequisites identified in some way? Horsti et al. were aware of business model frameworks consisting of many components and therefore looked also for differences between business model components concerning the identified prerequisites, but "no significant differences were found" (Horsti et al. 2005, p. 193). Key success factors needed to fulfill the stated prerequisites are:

- Integration of e-business into the firm's overall strategy

- Availability of suitable e-business skills

- High quality, reliability and usability of hard- and software

- Trust of customers and reputation

If e-business models are applied into a specific industry with specific competitors the key success factors may change. For example, for a cost driven company within the fashion industry cost reduction is a key success factor, so it would probably collaborate with an offshore business partner rather than build up own technology skills. A fashion company pursuing a differentiation strategy must be flexible, so it should collaborate with local business partners with global resourcing capabilities[5] to increase flexibility.

---

[4]Horsti et al. actually uses the terminology *critical success factors* following the definition by Rockart in the context of management information systems (Rockart 1979). Nevertheless Horsti et al. classify the critical success factors into *prerequisites of* and *measures of success*.

[5]*Global resourcing capabilities* describe the ability to produce world-wide, preferably in low-wage countries.

2.2 Fundamentals on virtual 3D worlds

In subsection 2.2.1 the character and features of virtual 3D worlds are examined. Subsection 2.2.2 describes two major forms of virtual worlds and compares them based on the virtual world value-chain. Key success factors for virtual world applications are discussed in 2.2.3.

2.2.1 Character and features of virtual 3D worlds

After defining and demarcating virtual worlds from online games, Web 2.0 applications and VR, the consumer characteristics are reviewed. Then market characteristics are depicted by introducing the virtual world value-chain. Concluding this subsection, the product life cycle of virtual worlds is examined.

2.2.1.1 Definition of the term *virtual 3D world*

The terminology for the object named *virtual 3D world* is not commonly agreed upon yet. IGDA[6] uses the term *persistent world* to emphasize the persistent nature[7] of these worlds (James et al. 2004). Castronova uses the term *synthetic world* to emphasize the synthetic nature of these worlds (Castronova 2005, p. 4-11). He does not use *virtual*, since this does resemble too much VR which is not the historical origin of virtual worlds, as discussed in this thesis (see also page 12). Nevertheless the author used *virtual 3D world*, because it best describes the research object by emphasizing the immersive character of those worlds. A summary definition might be:

> A virtual 3D world is a real-time persistent computer-based simulated three-dimensional environment, strongly encouraging user immersion. (Massively) multiple users can inhabit and interact in this environment via moving graphical user representations, called avatars. The presence awareness of other users is a key feature. Virtual 3D worlds do not have an in-world end state but are designed to go on forever.

---

[6]International Game Developers Association
[7]*Persistent* means that the world exists regardless if the consumer is logged into the world.

What *massively* means is still a point of discussion across experts. If it means *above 200 concurrent users per server*, then Second Life cannot be considered a virtual 3D world, since their maximum server capacity is currently 40 users (Rose 2007). The author understands *massively* as the number of concurrent users across all servers representing one instance of a virtual world. With this definition, Second Life is indeed massively, as areas are in principle accessible. To further refine the understanding of *virtual 3D worlds* in this thesis, the term is demarcated against Web 2.0, VR and the online gaming market.

Differences to Web 2.0 principles: The differences come from the inherent performance requirements regarding network and the processing power. For virtual worlds net latency requirements are prerequisites for success and require special programming currently not possible with the lightweight model[8] (Chen et al. 2006; Claypool and Claypool 2006; Brun et al. 2006). These requirements also prevent the access integration of other single devices in real-time. In contrast to Web 2.0, virtual worlds are more time consuming, making it very difficult to be in more than one virtual world actively, says Arc[9], a participant of MMORPGs for seven years. Virtual worlds also need a higher critical user mass than Web 2.0 applications to be economically successful, because they generally have higher development cost (James et al. 2004). Summing up, virtual worlds do have many commonalities to Web 2.0 applications, but they are also very different due to inherent performance requirements.

Differences to Virtual Reality: VR is the scientific development of the science fiction idea of *virtual reality*, which is colorfully described in novels like William Gibson's *Neuromancer* of 1984. Virtual worlds are the entertainment development of this idea. The difference lies in the approach to immersion: "the science program focused on sensory-input hardware, while gamers focused on mentally and emotionally engaging software" (Castronova 2005, p. 5). Despite these different approaches it cannot be ruled out, that the two could meet at some future time.

---

[8]The lightweight model refers to a technical client-server application architecture, where the client side is very small in size, resulting in lower client performance requirements.

[9]The complete interview with Arc can be found in appendix B.2.

Differences to the online gaming market: According to Martynow in addition
to virtual worlds this market encompasses other kinds of online games (Martynow 2007, pp. 23-38), beginning with games for short entertainment[10] to online
games like Blizzard's `www.battle.net`, where people around the world fight
each other in games like *Starcraft* for world championship (Wikipedia 2007d).
This makes virtual world just one particular type of online games.

2.2.1.2   Consumer characteristics

Virtual world consumer characteristics are important, as they are the basis for
product development and marketing. Whang and Chang did a lifestyle analysis
on consumers of the virtual world *Lineage*, which is one of the most successful
MMORPGs in Asia and particular in South Korea. They identified three online
lifestyles categories described in table 2.3 (Whang and Chang 2003).

The quotas are subject to *Lineage*, but the lifestyle types can be found in any

Lifestyle type	Description	Quota
Single-oriented	These players do not need to be part of some virtual community, but they also do not hinder other players to be what they like. For them virtual worlds are just bigger single player games. The community possibilities are of no interest to them.	28.2%
Community-oriented	Those players can be considered mainstream. They emphasize the community aspect and tend to follow hierarchical order. They are also very open-minded and real-life physical appearance and social group membership is of no concern to them.	44.8%
Off-real world type	Those players tend to show anti-social behavior within the virtual world. In-world success and materialistic values are important to them and they will do anything possible to achieve their goals, including joining communities, harming other players or cheating. They are most immersed into the virtual world compared to other lifestyle types.	26.9%

Table 2.3: Lifestyle categories of *Lineage* residents by Whang and Chang

virtual world.

---

[10]Examples can be found on `www.onlinespiele.org`

2.2.1.3 Market characteristics

The virtual world value-chain depicted in figure 2.2 was derived from sources used throughout this thesis. It represents the current state of deconstruction and focus on the product, disregarding chain links like distribution or customer service. Table 2.4 shows the five chain elements, their description and example companies.

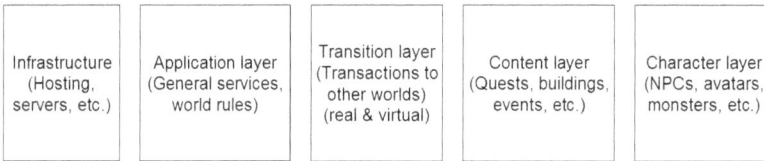

Infrastructure (Hosting, servers, etc.)	Application layer (General services, world rules)	Transition layer (Transactions to other worlds) (real & virtual)	Content layer (Quests, buildings, events, etc.)	Character layer (NPCs, avatars, monsters, etc.)

Figure 2.2: Virtual 3D world value-chain

Layer	Description	Company Example
Infrastructure	Infrastructure includes hosting, network support and such. It is basically the same as for normal business applications.	IBM, HP
Application	This is the virtual world itself, containing all general rules, services and user interfaces.	Sony Online Entertainment, Blizzard, Linden Lab
Transition	This layer includes all services, which connect virtual world among each other or to the real world.	Team VIP, Internet Gaming Entertainment
Content	The content layer includes all immobile in-world content, from landscape and buildings to missions or quests.	Blizzard, Sony Online Entertainment (SOE)
Character	The character layer includes the user avatars, computer-controlled non player characters and other movable objects.	SOE, Blizzard, Linden Lab

Table 2.4: Virtual 3D world value-chain elements

2.2.1.4 Product characteristics

The product life cycle of virtual worlds is similar to life cycles of other products, and can be mapped onto the five life cycle stages *development, introduction, growth, maturity* and *decline stage* (Kotler et al. 2005, pp. 604-609). Figure 2.3 shows the different stages and also the points of action and the actions used to maintain interest within the virtual world and to prevent it from entering the declining stage. The declining stage of virtual worlds ends with the stop of operations and thereby with the end of the virtual world. Three action types are important to maintain and grow virtual worlds (James et al. 2004, p. 66):

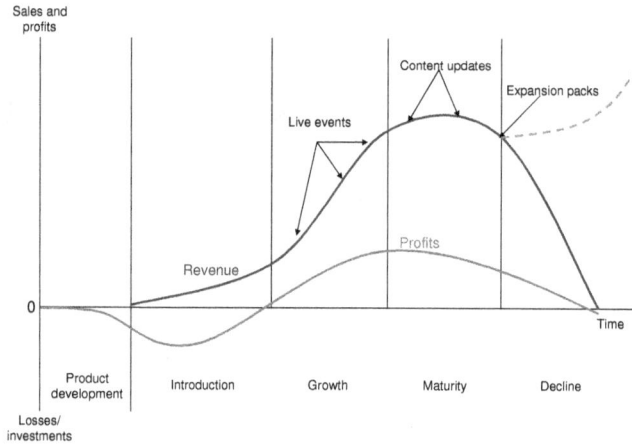

Figure 2.3: Product life cycle of virtual 3D worlds

- **Live events** are a relatively inexpensive type of action where people from the virtual world provider, for example developers, people from communication or marketing departments or management, enter the world for a specific time frame to lead some short event. Live events can also take a couple of hours or days, where the user is provided with special content or special situations. Live events increase the community feeling and help to grow and sustain the virtual world population by making the virtual world more interesting.

- **Content updates** are new content introductions at no extra charge for the consumers. Essentially for game worlds they are introduced in the maturity stage, to help retain the growing number of veteran users who have played through most of the content.

- **Expansion packs** are large amounts of content and features sold to old and new users. Whereas content updates are for every user, the extension pack content is only accessible for users, who buy it. Expansion packs are used when interest in the virtual world starts to decline to prevent a mass exodus of users which could end the virtual world. They are also used to attract new users.

2.2.2 Forms of virtual 3D worlds

Virtual worlds are also more generally called MMO[11] and come in many forms (cp. Wikipedia 2007b). The identified forms are mainly focused on *game types*, because virtual worlds originated from games. Although this segmentation is sensible for the gaming industry, it is insufficient for general business, as it gives the impression that virtual worlds are all about gaming, which is not the case.

In the course of his research the author came to the conclusion that the virtual world form should depend on the primary need of its target group. Considering this, nearly all identified *MMOxx*[12] types serve a target group which wants to be entertained. The author makes the following suggestion to classify virtual worlds from a general business perspective:

- **Entertainment virtual worlds** encompass all virtual worlds intended for gaming. Generally, these types of virtual worlds are called *MMORPG*, although the correct description should be *MMO*.

- **Community virtual worlds** include all kinds of virtual worlds, where communication and virtual community are the core. The world size is restricted and can be large or very small, as with the case of *3D chat-rooms*[13].

- **Business virtual worlds** encompass all virtual worlds, which are designed to further trading and the consumption of virtual goods or services.

These types determine the fundamental characteristics and in-world features of virtual worlds. In reality virtual worlds show the characteristics of hybrid types,

---

[11]Massively Multiplayer Online game

[12]For example: MMORPG, MMOFPS, MMOSG, etc. (cp. Wikipedia 2007b).

[13]There is a disagreement, if 3D environments like *IMVU 3D chat* should be seen as virtual world or only as 3D applications. Since the space IMVU offers, fits the definition on page 22, the author regards IMVU to be a virtual 3D world.

but the primary need served can always be associated to one type. For example, the primary need served by WoW[14] is entertainment, but it also holds community features and for Chinese *gold farmers* it is also about business. In the remainder of this subsection the entertainment and community types will be further described using case studies. The business type will be reviewed in section 2.3 using the case of Second Life.

2.2.2.1   The entertainment case: *World of Warcraft*

The characteristics and features for entertainment virtual worlds were deduced and verified by comparing the three MMORPGs *WoW*, *City of Heroes* and *Everquest II*[15].

Case: Blizzard Entertainment Inc. created WoW after its initial success with the *Warcraft* computer game trilogy. They implemented the subscription revenue model, where users get the first month free with the purchase of the software and then have to pay a monthly fee to be able to play. This is done by almost all entertainment virtual world providers. Like with all their game products, Blizzard emphasized the quality aspects in graphics, gameplay[16] and quality content. WoW is divided up into multiple identical worlds for performance reasons. Any transfer of characters or virtual goods between these worlds is not possible from within the worlds. The brand, the marketing and the high quality mentioned before led to their current position as the biggest MMORPG. After some content updates they introduced the first expansion pack, *The Burning Crusade*™, worldwide (except China) on January 16th this year and sold 2.4 million copies on the first 24 hours of availability (Blizzard Press Release 2007b). For consumers new to this world, they offer a 10-day free trial (Blizzard 2007).

Figures: WoW started in 2004 and has, as of July 24th, over nine million paying subscribers (Blizzard Press Release 2007a). Since the new expansion pack re-

---

[14]World of Warcraft

[15]A thorough statistical analysis on more than three MMOs would give more details but was out of scope for this thesis.

[16]*Gameplay* or *game mechanics* describe the interactive "look & feel" of virtual worlds, i.e. how good can the avatar be moved, how balanced is the fighting system, the in-world rules and such. It does not include graphics.

lease, for the U.S. and Europe only, WoW has around 0.8 million concurrent players online. This number is derived through a tool called *Warcraft CensusPlus UI Mod* which can be downloaded and installed into the game (WarcraftRealms.com 2007). It takes snapshots of the player's environment[17] which can be aggregated to provide the numbers outlined above.

Character and features: The following list of features defines an entertainment virtual world and can be found in WoW and other MMORPGs:

- *Avatar building* is one of the fundamental elements of entertainment worlds. This feature can be rather plain with a limited set of options, as in WoW, or it can be fully customizable, as in *City of Heroes/Villains*.

- *Level system* for recording avatar or player progress, i.e. improvements in fighting power, magic capability or constitution.

- *Fighting system* is a rule set which enables the avatar to use its skills to battle monsters or other avatars.

- *Missions* or *quests*, which have to be solved by the avatar to advance in the storyline. The solving of quests is normally rewarded with some sort of virtual value, like gold or items.

- *Exclusive regions* of the virtual world are restricted to avatars of a certain level or require the solving of a particular series of quests.

- *NPC*[18]*'s* or *monsters* take the role of the player adversary or in-world contact and are either part of some quest or just for increased challenge.

WoW does have many more features, including chat facilities, an auction house for in-world virtual goods trading, etc., but those features are not necessary requirements for an entertainment virtual world.

2.2.2.2 The community case: *Active Worlds*

The findings outlined below were deduced from research and verified by analyzing the community virtual worlds of *Active Worlds*.

---

[17]A player environment is defined by his faction, either *Horde* or *Alliance*, and the *realm* or server the player is logged into.

[18]Non Player Character

Case: Activeworlds Inc. created AW[19] in 1995, with the first world called *Alpha World*. Conceptually AW is a big group of private and public *worlds*, reachable through links called *teleports*. These worlds can be totally different, with different rules, graphics, intentions, etc. For example some of them are used for education, while others are for chatting and still others are for role-playing. Activeworlds implemented two revenue models: The first revenue model is B2B and addresses companies, universities or individuals, who want to own and build a world. They have different pricing depending on server size, number of concurrent users and public accessibility (Activeworlds 2007b). They also have special pricing for educational classes directed at universities or companies (Activeworlds 2007a). The second revenue model is B2C. Users can access AW without subscription, but central features are available only through a monthly subscription. Although AW has existed since 1997, it is not as prominent as *WoW* or *SL*, because it is neither as successful as WoW, nor is it as hyped as SL.

Figures: According to Activeworlds Inc. information AW has 2 million users from which 70,000 are paying subscribers. Since the beginning they have had 362,105 citizens[20]. There are currently 741 accessible private and public worlds. As Activeworlds also sells servers without connection to the main server cluster, there could be even more implementations. There is no statistical information available for number of concurrent users over the past 30 days. On July, 27th at 22:00 German time, there were a total of 186 users online. This figure is by no means representative, but nevertheless shows the order of magnitude.

Character and features: The following list of features defines a community type virtual world and can be found in AW and other community type virtual worlds:

- *Differentiation between public and private space* so that communities have the freedom to choose, whether they admit outsiders.

- *Differentiation based on content rating*, i.e. AW worlds are rated G, PG, PG-13, R and X[21].

---

[19]Active Worlds

[20]This is the citizen number assigned to the author. This number also includes citizens, who just take the free trial week, so no conclusions can be made rearing subscriber numbers.

[21]Rating is based on the U.S. film rating system. The levels are: G – General audiences, PG –

- *Chat facilities* which can be either broadcast, so everyone can listen, or peer-to-peer, called *whisper*.

- *Asynchronous communication* in-world, much like email. In AW they are called *telegram*.

- *Friends list*, so people can remember likable persons inside the virtual world.

- *Virtual community membership*, so a user can show that he belongs to a certain group of users.

- *Graphical building facilities* including landscape, buildings and to some extent avatars. AW has all options, although avatar modeling is restricted to the world owner to guarantee world theme consistence.

AW does not include gaming or business services naturally, but each owner is allowed to create his own rules and do, what he likes, says Ariadne[22], world owner of *Crete*, a world themed around ancient Minoan culture.

2.2.3   Success factors of virtual 3D world applications

All key success factors of e-business models listed on page 21 are also valid for the success of e-business models based on virtual world applications. Additional to these, there were also specific prerequisites of success found through the interviews in appendix B, concerning mainly the overall performance of a virtual world application.

- *Visual quality of graphics:* The visual graphics quality is not the same as *realistic* graphics. Graphics have to look good and they must be consistent in themselves, i.e. it should not be possible to look through the edges of a house.

- *Graphic engine performance:* The engine rendering performance determines the immersion factor of the world. If the graphic quality is good, but the rendering speed is poor, virtual world immersion will suffer.

Parental guidance suggested, PG-13 – Parents strongly cautioned, R – Restricted and X (same as NC-17) – No one 17 and under admitted (Wikipedia 2007c).

[22]The complete interview with Ariadne can be found in appendix B.5.

- *Server performance:* Reliability, server response time and server capacity are key to server performance, i.e. if concurrent user capacity is too low, the virtual world looses attractiveness compared to other e-business solutions.

- *Network performance:* Broadband bandwidth access increases, as will be seen on page 43. This fact must be used by virtual worlds. If customers have broadband access, they also want to use it, so virtual worlds must leverage this.

- *Overall scalability:* The virtual world has to be scalable in terms of soft- and hardware to accommodate increasing user numbers. If this is done poorly, the existing users will suffer and ultimately leave the virtual world.

- *Creative capabilities:* are also very important. There is no point in a scalable stable high-performance virtual world, if the user cannot creatively express in any form, i.e. avatar modification or building virtual objects.

Considering those prerequisites of virtual world application success, the following additional key success factors can be derived:

- **Software innovation capability:** Virtual world must differentiate to become successful. Therefore the companies have to innovate regarding virtual world features as well as provide an environment, where users are enabled to innovate themselves.

- **Availability of art skills:** The emphasis to graphics requires companies to have art skills available, additional to e-business skills. As with e-business skills, the art skills can also be outsourced of course.

- **High performance of hard- and software:** Considering that virtual worlds should serve massively numbers of concurrent users they must be designed for high performance and run on high performance hardware. Any trade-off in this aspect endangers success.

These basic key success factors do not secure overall virtual world success. They are complemented by virtual world type dependent in-world key success factors, which will be addressed in subsection 3.2.2.

2.3 Fundamentals on Second Life

Second Life from Linden Research Inc. is a business type virtual world. Although it is not the only virtual world, explicitly furthering real currency trading, it is the only one with the clear primary intention to do so. In the case of *Entropia Universe* from MindArk the primary intention is not so clear on first sight due to its stronger hybrid approach. It is a business virtual world, but with some differences to SL[23], which are discussed in subsection 2.3.2.

The introduction of SL starts with the available figures on SL and Linden Research. Then the characters and features of SL were examined, before the value propositions of SL were scrutinized in subsection 2.3.3.

2.3.1 Figures on Linden Research Inc. and *Second Life*

Linden Research Inc. figures: Linden Research Inc. is a privately held company, founded in 1999 by Philip Rosedale. The name *Linden Lab* seems to be the brand of *Linden Research Inc.*, so they are used interchangeably, for example in the TOS[24] or on the websites. In 2004 LL[25] had 31 employees and was largely owned by a handful of key corporate investors[26] (Linden Research Inc. 2004). The number of employees increased to about 140 in 2007, according to *USA Today* (cited in Wikipedia 2007a). Until at least the first quarter 2006 Philip Rosedale admitted, that LL was not yet profitable (Hof 2006).

Second Life figures: SL was launched in June 2003 as commercial online service. The 7.7 million registrations in June 2007 represent 5.2 million unique users or *residents*. Of those, 94,607 are paying subscribers (see Linden Research Inc. 2007a, Key metrics: excel format link). In June over 99% of the residents online were over 18 years old, compared to the industry average of 69% referred to on page 42. SL has an average of 10,000 to 45,000 concurrent residents at different

---

[23]Second Life
[24]Terms of Service
[25]Linden Lab
[26]Named institutional investors are Kapor Enterprises, Catamount Ventures, Benchmark Capital and Omidyar Network. A newer source (Hof 2006) adds also Globespan Capital Partners to the list. Additionally to those institutional investors, there are also big private investors, namely Jeffrey P. Bezos, CEO and founder of Amazon, as well as Apple, Bank of America and Goldman Sachs current and former executives.

times of day.

The comparison of those figures with that of entertainment typed virtual worlds is difficult as the underlying revenue model is different. The primary revenue model for most entertainment virtual worlds is subscriptions, whereas SL's revenue model is based more on services provided, like *renting in-world land*[27].

With the data provided by LL through their website (Linden Research Inc. 2007a, Key metrics: excel format) the continuous monthly revenue for June, excluding one-time revenue streams like selling of new land, can be approximated to $4.3 million:

- *Revenue through subscription*: 94,607 subscribers at an average subscription fee of $7.50 per month[28] minus L$1200, at an average sell-rate of L$277 : $1 which is granted from LL for premium accounts, they made net revenue of about **$300,000**.

- *Revenue through maintenance fees for islands*: In June SL hosted 546.01 km^2 island land; with a maintenance fee of $4,501 per km^2 they made revenue of about **$2.46 million**.

- *Revenue through usage fees for mainland*: This is not easily approximated, as the usage fee depends on the land size and the size distribution is not available. This revenue could be anything from **$0.5 to $1.6 million**.

- *Revenue from other activities*: LL also makes revenue through fees on currency exchange, uploads, directory listings, group creation, etc. All this can be approximated to about **$0.53 million**.

Obviously revenue from subscriptions contributes only about 7% of total revenue. If the June sale revenue of new islands of around $1.55 million is also taken into account, subscriptions amount to only 5% of the revenue. This is of interest, since it puts the Internet discussions about *total residents, concurrent residents* and their comparisons to WoW numbers into the right perspective: Comparing the total revenue per month, WoW is making about $126 million[29] recurring rev-

---

[27]Land renting in SL is the same as hosting web space with a services package, like for example the European Internet service provider *HostEurope* does. In this sense *islands* and *mainland* are in-world SL terms for private and public web space.

[28]For a quarterly subscription

[29]Roughly approximated with 9 million subscribers paying an average of $14 per month. The rates are geography dependant (Wikipedia 2007e).

enue per month compared to approximately \$4.3 million. Subscription numbers cannot be compared, as the revenue business model is different.

2.3.2   Character and features of Second Life

Similar to other virtual world implementations, Second Life is also a hybrid solution. To obtain a complete picture of SL features belonging to entertainment or community virtual worlds will also be described.

Business virtual world features: The following list of features can be found in SL and other business virtual worlds.

- *Virtual currency* is needed to conduct virtual business in-world. This could also be done using regular currency. Virtual currency has the advantage of giving the freedom of arbitrary value setting to the virtual world provider.

- *Trading and market system* are needed to support virtual transactions between participants or between participants and the environment.

- *Official exchange rates* separate the business virtual world implementation from implementations of currency and economic systems in entertainment worlds. In the business case the exchange rates make it possible to convert virtual currency into real currency and vice versa, thereby offering the possibility to realize real profits. This feature can be extended into a full *Micro e-payment system*, as in the EU[30] case. Virtual worlds have a trust-advantage compared to the Internet, where micro e-payment systems never took off (Tan 2004, p. 177), since there is only one institution defining the currency.

- *Rules of ownership* determine what electronic state means *owning* something in a virtual world and what not. Here it is important to point out that *in-world owning* does not necessarily match the legal meaning of owning in the real world. MindArk for example excludes all forms of real ownership on virtual goods in its EULA[31], although in-world users own their goods virtually (MindArk PE AB 2007a, chapter 7: Ownership).

---

[30]Entropia Universe
[31]End User License Agreement

- *Security of financial information* must be on the level maintained by financial institutes, since the objects of action are currency, accounts and financial transactions. This point is not yet implemented to full extent in SL. A prove for this claim can be found within the law case mentioned on page 40. Before getting expropriated by LL, the accuser utilized a technical exploit and bought auction land on low prices before the auctions even started. This he did with directly typing the URL[32] address into the auction system of SL, a well known hacking technique normally blocked in business applications (Pendragon 2007).

What can be observed here is that the first two features are also used in the context of in-world economy systems of entertainment worlds. The *official exchange rates* feature is transforming a virtual world into a business type. Once this transformation is done, the other two features become mandatory consequences.

Other SL features: Additionally to the business type features, SL does have entertainment and community features. The implementation of the *avatar building* entertainment feature in SL is theoretically without limit. In reality the basic options are very limited and everything else needs a technology savvy user to create and upload avatar items. In comparison to this, the feature implementation in *City of Heroes/Villains* is usable for all participants with the skill to click buttons. With the exception of the *differentiation based on content rating* feature, SL implements all community features described on page 30. The missing feature is only rudimentary implemented in SL in the sense, that there is a SL for adults and a SL for teenagers.

Comparing SL to EU: There are not many business virtual world implementations (yet). Second Life and Entropia Universe are two current instances of this type, although there are differences. EU includes entertainment features additional to *avatar building*, making it more appealing to player consumers. On the other side, it is more restrictive on *rules of ownership*, claiming all IP[33] rights of user creations or actions. In contrast to this, SL does recognize the IP rights of

---

[32]Uniform Resource Locator
[33]Intellectual Property

residents. EU is more advanced in the implementation of the *official exchange rates* feature, as well as the *security of financial information* feature, which emphasizes its business nature. In August this year, MindArk will ship the first *Entropia Universe Cash Cards* usable "to pay [with in-world currency] for goods and services in retail outlets, or to withdraw real cash from millions of ATM[34] machines around the world" (MindArk PE AB 2007b), while implementing security systems comparable to online banks.

2.3.3   Value propositions of Second Life

SL offers B2B and B2C services and provides a platform for C2C transactions. Taking the revenue model into account it can be seen, that LL emphasizes B2B value propositions more than B2C.

B2C – Value proposition toward consumers: The value proposition toward consumers is the same, as in all virtual worlds: Immersion and entertainment in a virtual world, meeting new people in virtual communities and being creative. The last point is emphasized in SL, as SL offers all consumers a space, where they can be as creative as they like with minimal technical restrictions.   The entertainment part comes more from the *creative* and *community* aspects, than from the pure *game* aspect, as SL does not have any entertainment features needed for games, such as *missions* or *quests*, although they can be created by residents (Deep Blue Book 2007, video clip 11 to 13).

The attractiveness of this value proposition is not easy to deduce. Taking Ariadne as example, it would be attractive, as creativity and building are most important for her. On the other hand, participants like Arc are not attracted at all, as SL is a virtual world without any goal or direction. *Creativity* is expressed by consumers like Arc through mastering difficult in-world situations, rather than designing things. This divide could be found in numerous forum contributions or web logs: Either consumers wanted to express themselves creatively through designing objects, or they wanted to have a goal or a direction.

---

[34]Automated Teller Machine

B2B – Value proposition toward businesses: Four major value propositions can be identified for B2B:

- *Virtual business platform:* Directed toward individuals as well as corporations, SL offers the possibility to trade and make money through virtual goods sold to consumers inside SL.

- *Education platform:* Directed toward corporations as well as education organizations, SL, like AW, offers a space for education as 3D advancement of current e-learning solutions.

- *Marketing platform:* Directed toward marketing analysts and marketing departments, SL offers a space, where "tech-savvy and fashion-forward consumers [. . .] are flocking to [join] these *avant-garde* virtual communities, [. . .]" (Berman et al. 2007, p. 22).

- *Community platform:* Directed toward corporations, SL offers a gathering place for highly educated participants, from which corporations can recruit the talents of tomorrow.

Some of those value propositions can also be found in AW, like the *education* and *community* platform value proposition. The *marketing* and *virtual business* platform value propositions are business virtual world specific. The attractiveness of SL as a marketing platform seems inferior in comparison to *Google Earth* or *Virtual Earth* from Microsoft, because the later two have clear connections to reality in terms of geography. The attractiveness of SL as virtual business platform on the other hand is high, because the value proposition is innovative and at this point in time still unique in the offered breadth.

Chapter 3

The attractiveness of virtual 3D worlds for business

In section 1.1 the author argued for attractiveness of virtual worlds, based on the hypothesis, that a three-dimensional user interface is more accessible than the two-dimensional interface used throughout the Internet. Looking at different virtual worlds one can see, that *3D* is the only recurring characteristic of user interfaces. Castronova even argued, that because virtual worlds "are among the most intensive applications [...] there is a steep learning curve using them" (Castronova 2005, p. 132). This shows that even if 3D user interfaces are generally more accessible, their implementation as of today is not yet on the required level. If 3D user interfaces are not mature today, why should a company outside the entertainment industry start to think about investing in virtual 3D worlds? Why are those worlds attractive? To answer these questions, the attractiveness of virtual 3D worlds for business was explored.

In section 3.1 the macro environmental changes and the resulting threats and opportunities pertaining virtual worlds were examined. Since in-world key success factors depend on the virtual world type, a segmentation analysis of the virtual world industry was conducted in section 3.2. Finally in section 3.3 the recent deconstruction of the virtual world value-chain was examined at the case examples described in chapter 2, in order to identify new business opportunities.

3.1   Macro environmental changes and virtual worlds

With the increased popularity of virtual worlds, macro environmental changes took place which is the subject of this section. The macro environmental factors were analyzed in subsection 3.1.1 using the PEST analysis approach described in appendix A.2. The results were evaluated in subsection 3.1.2 by comparing their impact on virtual world business in comparison to their uncertainty degree.

3.1.1   Analysis of macro environmental factors

Political and legal factors: Because of the immersive nature of virtual worlds young adults are endangered of becoming addicted to these worlds, neglecting their real lives. In Asia this situation urged governments to adapt legislation to protect the youth and thereby future economic growth (Chai 2003; Dickie 2005; Xing 2007). These problems are not specific Asian, as the opening of a game-addict clinic in Amsterdam demonstrates (Thorsen 2006). With the rise of business virtual worlds, legal factors came up, which have to be resolved (Lober 2007; Trantow 2007):

- **Criminal law** is faced with graphical animated representation. For example a German television report investigation showed SL residents involved in the role plays of pedophilia with explicit sexual violence acts (Dauser and Schader 2007). Is such role play subject to freedom of speech or a criminal act? How is ethic affected by the increasing graphical possibilities in the future? Those questions cannot be answered easily.

- **Right of ownership** and liability in virtual worlds is not clear. Although providers like LL do leave the copyright to the customer, they undermine his right of ownership. As Example, Marc Bragg was expropriated of his SL virtual property by LL through cancellation of his account (Trantow 2007; Parlow 2007).

- **Liability** for lost virtual goods, due to technical failures or security leaks, although explicitly excluded in virtual world EULAs is not clear. Courts already ruled in favor of consumers (MacInnes and Hu 2005, p. 196; Chosun-ilbo 2006).

- **Tax policy** is adapted to virtual goods trading, because real income can be generated. U.S. congress and other governments are currently analyzing the situation (Bonacker 2007; Schoolmann 2007).

Economic factors: A distinction has to be made concerning economic factors affecting the virtual world industry and in-world economic factors. One economic factor relevant for v-business may become unemployed people with their available time resources. They could easily waste their resources on virtual worlds by just escaping from their real-world problems. On the other hand they could leverage the available resources and launch their own v-business world-wide, circumventing the financial risk of doing business in the real world. The new economy of virtual asset trading is predicted by IGE[1] to reach $7 billion by 2009 (IGE.com 2007). The *value* of those virtual goods is affected primarily by the virtual economic factors within virtual worlds which are in principal decoupled from real world economic factors.

On the supply side virtual world providers can adjust the exchange rates and the money volume within virtual worlds anytime without having to justify themselves to any government or bank organization. This fact is important, because through the exchange rates into the real world, this behavior can actually affect economic factors in the real world or make a v-business model unattractive. For example Dibbell claimed in his article about Chinese *Gold Farmers*, that 100 WoW gold coins could be exchanged to about $20 (Dibbell 2007). A quick research of the author and statements of guild members[2] revealed that in August, just two months after the article release, the mean value for 100 gold coins dropped to about 1.65 €. This drop is attributed by players to the new expansion set of WoW which devalued gold in a fundamental way [3].

On the demand side virtual world participants can leave the world, heralding the end of its life cycle and rendering all virtual goods worthless[4].

---

[1] Internet Gaming Entertainment

[2] A guild is a form of an in-world virtual community. Guilds can be either informal or very active with real world meetings, own web-pages and a hierarchy.

[3] The devaluation was not direct, but rather it became much easier to accumulate 100 gold coins in the new areas, than in the initial areas of the world.

[4] The real world example would be some country, which ends and vanishes, like the historical Inca Empire, with the minor difference, that all Inca gold and South American land owned by someone would disintegrate into electrons at the same time.

Social factors: Social studies in the past years have observed three effects introduced by the Internet, which changed with the emergence of virtual worlds:

- **Free communication with new constrains:** Text-based Internet communication is free of social cues or social group membership (Guadagno and
  Cialdini 2005). Virtual worlds reintroduce *physical* appearance and social
  group membership in the form of the virtual self, or *avatar*. Although ano-
  nymity still exists, the virtual appearance introduces a new kind of prejudices based on the virtual appearance.

- **Pro-social behavior:** Internet already boosted pro-social behavior through
  increased schedule flexibility and convenience (Sproull et al. 2005). Virtual
  worlds can further stimulate this trend, as possible benefits can also be seen
  outside the own community (i.e. graphical badges) which in turn increases
  reputation, one of the main drivers for pro-social behavior.

- **Dissolution of gender behavior and hardening of stereotypes:** Schaap
  (2006) and O'Riordan (2006) both describe the notion of *gender* online. While
  the avatar's gender does not imply the user real gender, the virtual representation of gender becomes more stereotyped. This development is further
  augmented by virtual worlds and may lead to unrealistic standards concerning feminine beauty, manhood or expected gender behavior patterns.

The social implications of MMORPGs are big enough that *Game Studies* are described as an emerging new research field within social studies (Aarseth 2006). In
2001 "the average age of videogame players is 28" (Newman 2004, p. 50) according to IDSA[5] renamed into ESA[6] in 2003. According to latest data, the average
age of players increased to 33 years, with 69% being over 18 and 25% being over
50 years old (ESA 2007).

Fung examined the connection life in virtual gaming worlds has to the real life
and "argues for the impossibility of disconnecting the cyberworld from the real
world when the online setting (e.g., gaming) is basically dictated by, delimited
by, or modeled from real-world settings" (Fung 2006, p. 138).

This could make virtual worlds irreplaceable network places in a fast and flexi-

---

[5]Interactive Digital Software Association
[6]Entertainment Software Association

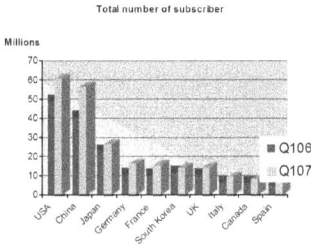

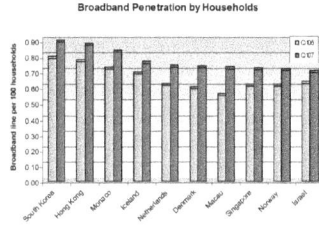

Figure 3.1: Top 10 broadband countries by number of lines

Figure 3.2: Top 10 broadband countries by household penetration

(Both diagrams source: Point Topic 2007)

bility demanding economy. They are a major improvement compared to email or chat rooms, as textual information is "a medium with low social presence[7]" (Koh et al. 2007). People can acquire new *shared experiences*, like storming a castle in WoW (Billhardt 2007) or participating in a beauty contest in SL.

Technological factors: There are three technological trends, which enable wider spread of virtual worlds. The **worldwide increase of bandwidth** is one prerequisite for virtual worlds. Point Topic observed in its recent broadband report, that the worldwide total of broadband lines reached 298,1 million in the first quarter of 2007 (Point Topic 2007), representing a year-on-year growth rate of 28.7%[8].

Figure 3.1 shows that although USA is still the country with most broadband lines, China is set to overtake the U.S. in terms of total number of lines. Figure 3.2 shows that according to household penetration, South Korea is nearly fully saturated with 89.4%. These figures are reflected also by the spread of virtual world users, as virtual worlds need broadband access.

The second trend is the **worldwide increase of processing power**. On the client side the *graphics-processing unit* market for consumer graphic cards is dominated by U.S. based Nvidia Corporation and Canada based ATI Technologies acquired by AMD Inc. in 2006. This market has increased steadily over the past few years

---

[7]"Social presence, or the degree to which the medium facilitates awareness of other people and interpersonal relationships during interaction, is critical for effective communications in many social/work contexts."(Koh et al. 2007, p. 70)

[8]For a report focused on Germany and its position within the worldwide broadband market see Graumann and Neinert (2004).

due to growing popularity of video games in general (Geer 2006). On the server side virtual worlds are also initiating new developments and ideas. IBM for example announced an upgrade of its mainframe systems with the new Cell processor to cope with the processing power demand of virtual worlds (IBM 2007a). The third trend is the **increase of access ease**. Recent developments for consumers, like the 3D navigation controller described by Cass show that user interfaces are already influenced by the increased popularity of the third dimension (Cass 2007). On the vendor side the development and maintenance ease of virtual world software is supported by highly sophisticated development environments extended to harbor also digital art and optimized hardware environments. The ACM[9] dedicated a *queue* magazine issue in 2004, describing the complexity of the game development process in more detail (Grossmann, ed 2004).

3.1.2   Evaluation of macro environmental factors

The factors identified in subsection 3.1.1 are evaluated as opportunities or threats in table 3.1. Their relevance is assessed based on their estimated impact on virtual world business models and their probability of occurrence (see figure 3.3). Political factors are colored blue, economic yellow, social green and technological gray. Opportunities are marked with capital letters and circles whereas threats are marked with small letters and squares.

All identified political factors pose threats to virtual world business models. Of them, p_3 and p_4 are the biggest threats, because they will certainly occur and they affect ownership and liability. Taxation poses a medium risk, because it can be mitigated quite simple. From the economic factors only e_3 seems to be a probable threat. With entertainment virtual worlds the probability of e_2 increases, as the in-world economic system is not designed for real business and therefore has no implied restrictions on the vendor's arbitrariness. From the social factors only the increasing average age (S_4) is an opportunity to bear in mind during planning. The impact of s_1 is not clear, as people will still have more possibilities to belong to the new social groups, despite real social cues or social group belonging. All technological factors are almost certain to happen and open new opportunities.

---

[9]Association for Computing Machinery

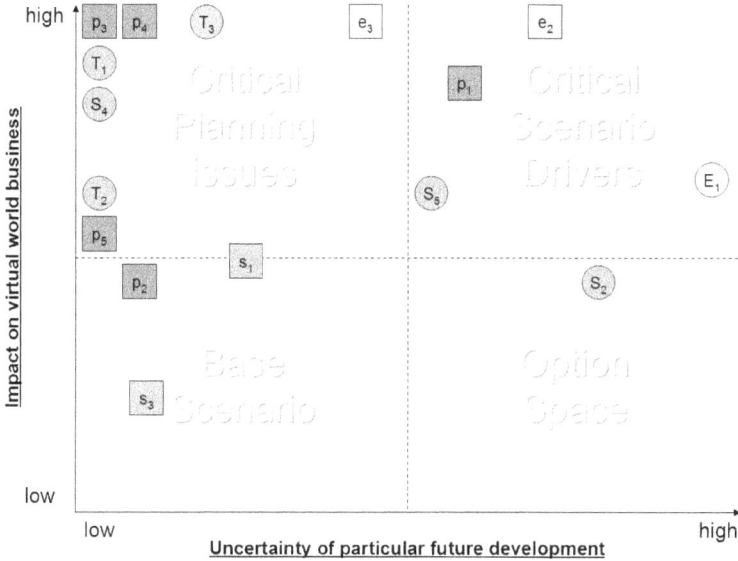

Figure 3.3: Impact-uncertainty assessment of macro environmental factors

O/T	Description of macro environmental factor
p_1	Threat of over regulation, due to danger of youth addiction
p_2	Threat of bad reputation, due to criminal or ethical ambiguities
p_3	Threat of investment loss, due to unclear ownership rights
p_4	Threat of investment loss, due to insufficient liability clarity
p_5	Threat of financial risk, due to unclear taxation responsibilities
E_1	Opportunity of increased virtual world population
e_2	Threat of supply side changes of the virtual economic system
e_3	Threat of demand side pullout of the virtual world
s_1	Threat of social bias in communication, due to avatar appearance
S_2	Opportunity of increased prosocial behavior, due to recognition
s_3	Threat of gender bias due to one sided graphical avatar appearance
S_4	Opportunity of management involvement because of user age
S_5	Opportunity of intensified networking, due to shared experiences
T_1	Opportunity of increased market accessibility through broadband connectivity growth
T_2	Opportunity of lowered technical access barriers, due to increased computing power
T_3	Opportunity of lower development cost through sophisticated hard- and software

Table 3.1: Macro economic opportunities and threats

3.2   Virtual world industry segmentation

The macro environment analysis in the preceding section showed that opportunities accrue from the rise of virtual worlds, which companies can leverage to their advantage. Virtual 3D worlds exist in many forms, as was already shown in subsection 2.2.2. The customer groups targeted are different for each form, as well as production requirements and development or maintenance cost. To analyze the current and possible future forms of virtual worlds a segmentation analysis was conducted.

In subsection 3.2.1 the segmentation variables for the virtual world industry are identified to construct the segmentation matrix, while the in-world segment specific key success factors are described in subsection 3.2.2.

3.2.1   Identification of virtual world segmentation variables

The segmentation variables were defined by examining buyers as well as products. From the candidate variables three were chosen based on their perceived impact on industry structure and competitive advantage strategies (Porter 1985, p. 234). The following variables were chosen to construct the 3D segmentation matrix in figure 3.4:

Customer group focus: Virtual world buyers can be classified according to their primary need or focus, when choosing a virtual world to participate in. The groups defined have to be marketed differently and the virtual world production differs also, because the key characteristics differ, as will be shown later.
As was already shown on page 27, this segmentation variable segments the virtual world industry into the three segments *entertainment*, *community* and *business* virtual worlds.

Virtual world openness: This variable is a combination of buyer and product characteristics. Virtual worlds can be used for B2C as well as B2B e-business models. The ability, just how much B2B business is possible is determined by the virtual world openness. From the product perspective this variable determines the financial and technical resources and capabilities needed to build the virtual world and depends on the value-chain coverage of the product[10].

The virtual world industry is segmented based on the virtual world value chain depicted in figure 2.2. The *infrastructure layer* is neglected in this discussion, as it does not affect the in-world openness of the virtual world.

- **Closed:** Virtual world vendor controls $\geq 90\%$ of the value-chain.

- **Restricted:** Virtual world vendor controls $\geq 75\%$ of the value-chain.

- **Open:** Virtual world vendor controls $\geq 50\%$ of the value-chain.

- **Unrestricted:** Virtual world vendor controls $< 50\%$ of the value-chain.

Control in this context means that the vendor creates the controlled value without partners. For example, WoW leaves little room for world participants to change or influence the virtual world and can be considered a *closed* world, whereas SL is an *unrestricted* virtual world.

Virtual world theme: The virtual world theme is a product characteristic, which to some extent constrains the applicability of B2B e-business models. For example *IBM blade server* marketing would not fit into a fantasy themed virtual world, regardless how open it is. If the product would be *replica swords* or *horse riding lessons*, they would fit the fantasy setting. It also determines the private buyer target group: Consumers interested in *science fiction* would not enter a *fantasy* virtual world.

There are many possible segments in this variable. Some examples are *fantasy*, *science fiction, present day, superheroes* or *Looney Toons*. This segmentation variable should not be confused with **virtual world graphic style**, where possible segments would be *realistic* or *comic*. The customer preference of the graphic style is minor compared to the theme. For example fantasy enthusiasts would probably join *Everquest II* as easily as *WoW*, although they have different graphic styles.

Segmentation matrix of virtual world industry: The resulting segmentation matrix is shown in figure 3.4, with the classification of the virtual worlds discussed so far.

---

[10]The smallest coverage of the value-chain depicted in figure 2.2, which can be considered a virtual world, is the *application layer*. The vertical segmentation depicted in figure 4.1 results into *technical* virtual world *parts*, which have to be integrated to become a minimal virtual world.

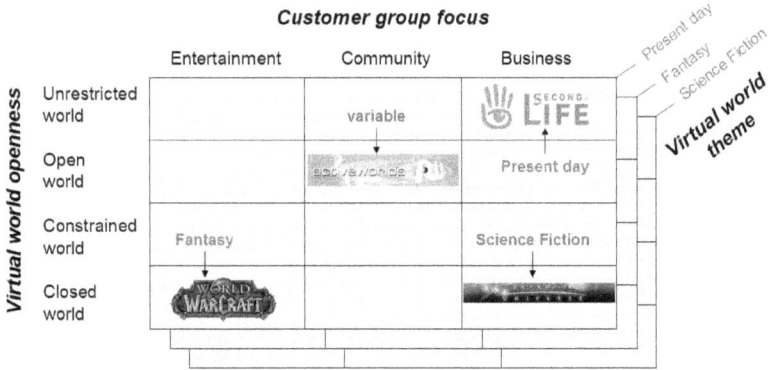

Figure 3.4: Segmentation matrix of virtual world industry

3.2.2   Success factors in virtual 3D world segments

The key success factors in subsection 2.2.3 are valid for all virtual world applications, regardless of the segment they are in. The in-world key success factors are partly subject to the virtual world segment. Below the five key success factors, derived from research and the interviews conducted, are introduced:

- **High immersion factor to increase customer loyalty:** The immersion factor of the world is the degree, to which the user is enabled to immerse into the virtual world. Aspects, which further this factor, are a *virtually endless world*, a *consistent graphical setting* and the *storyline*, especially in MMORPGs. To simulate a living world, there also has to be some sort of *in-world growth of experience*.

- **No creativity restrictions, to allow user self expression:** Virtual worlds are spaces, where people like the *freedom of choice* to do, what they can't do in the real world. MMORPGs for example do not have one specific storyline, like games, but offer multiple concurrent stories, the user can choose from, so he can *develop his avatar* as he likes. Other virtual worlds, like AW or SL, allow the user to express himself by *building* virtual objects. *New content* is in this regard important, as it teases the user to explore.

- **Design virtual world to provide flow experience:** Happiness and fun, described in positive psychology with the *flow concept*, is a function of the challenge an environment represents and the user's ability. The challenge should not be too high as it increases user anxiety and not to low as it bores the user (Chen 2007). Factors supporting flow experience are the *user interface*, the *in-world rules*, *the game balance* and the overall handling or *gameplay*.

- **Superior virtual community management:** The attractiveness of virtual worlds depends, due to their interactive nature, strongly on the quality of their *virtual community*. The community management must take the *customer characteristics* presented on page 24 into account. To devise a good community strategy, the *user type quotas* for the own virtual world must be well known.

- **High level of privacy and in-world security systems:** Privacy and security is critical for success of e-business applications in general, so for business virtual worlds this is important. When corporate customers start using virtual worlds as meeting places, these meetings must be secure, so no external person can listen to confidential information. Also transactions of virtual goods or currency exchange must be secured against fraud attempts.

Those key success factors do not have the same impact on all customer group segments, as figure 3.5 shows. The relevance was derived through a qualitative analysis of the expert interviews. Details and the approach taken can be found in appendix B.1.

For example, the *immersion factor* is very important for the entertainment segment. If immersion is low, the whole world is unattractive. Another example would be the *flow experience*, which has medium impact on business virtual worlds. In business applications the *usability* is sometimes an issue, but the trade-off between effort and benefit to reach a high level of *flow* is not positive for e-business solutions. With virtual world business solutions, *flow* has to be considered, but not to the same degree, as in games.

A deeper analysis on the business world segment revealed, that the impact of those key success factors, and thereby the needed degree for success, is also influenced by the *virtual world openness*, as can be seen in figure 3.6[11]. *Normal effort*

---

[11]The analogue figures for the entertainment or community segments are of course different, since the effort increase/degrease is relative to the initial impact of the success factor in the particular segment.

Customer group focus

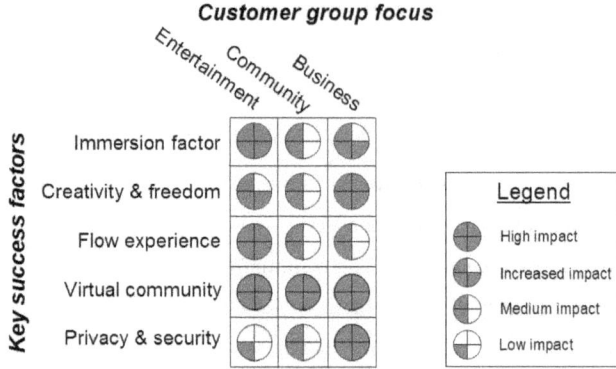

Figure 3.5: Impact of in-world success factors on virtual 3D world segments

describes the effort needed to implement a viable solution corresponding to impact degree of the particular success factor. The other effort degrees are relative to normal effort.

For example, in an unrestricted business virtual world the effort to reach the *immersion factor* degree needed (see figure 3.5), will probably increase, while it would decrease for restricted or closed virtual worlds, since the company controls more of the value-chain in those cases. Another example is *privacy and security*. It is more complex to guarantee privacy and security within an unrestricted or open virtual world, because they inherently have many public interfaces, which increase the probability of security leaks.

Business virtual world openness

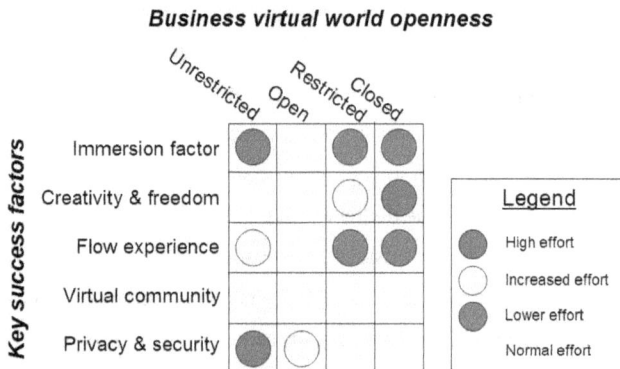

Figure 3.6: Success factor implementation effort relative to openness degree

3.3 Business model overview for virtual 3D worlds

The preceding section showed that virtual worlds offer business opportunities also outside the gaming industry. The next step is to identify business models applicable onto virtual worlds. For this step, the systematic approach used by Timmers, which is "based on value-chain deconstruction and reconstruction – that is, identifying value-chain elements – and identifying possible ways of integrating information along the value-chain"(Timmers 2000, p. 33), was used.

First the virtual world openness degree implemented by the companies described in chapter 2 was analyzed, utilizing the virtual world value-chain depicted in figure 2.2. Based on this analysis three generic business models are identified for deeper analysis in chapter 4.

3.3.1 Comparative analysis based on the value-chain

The strategy companies implemented through deconstructing the value-chain pertaining virtual 3D worlds was examined by comparing WoW against AW in figure 3.7 and EU against SL in figure 3.8.

Comparing WoW with AW: WoW is a good example for entertainment virtual worlds, since the only actors allowed are either infrastructure partners or the world participants. Due to the fact that graphic engine performance is a key success factor for virtual 3D worlds (see subsection 2.2.3), both, Blizzard and Activeworlds, did not outsource any part of the application layer, as this would mean less differentiation from competitors. In comparison to the entertainment segment, the community segment shows, at the example of AW, a shift of c.1 to e.1 towards the infrastructure layer. This can also be seen in the revenue model.

Companies in the entertainment segment are concerned about subscription numbers, whereas companies in the community segment generate revenue also as service providers, selling their application layer, and the server needed to run them, to prospective world owners, be they private persons, like Ariadne, or big corporations like Siemens. It is noteworthy here that AW, just as SL, focuses also on the education value proposition.

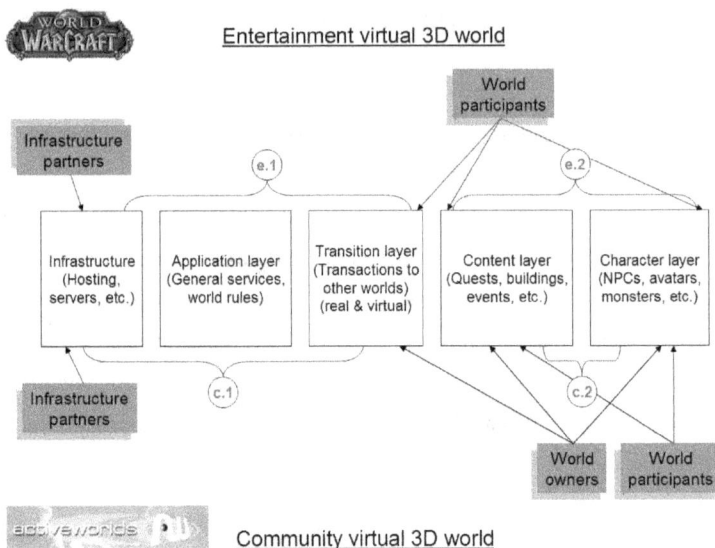

Figure 3.7: Value-chain based comparison of WoW against AW

Comparing EU with SL: Figure 3.8 shows two things: The first one is that business virtual worlds collaborate with service providers or partners to enhance the transition layer, i.e. currency exchange services[12], or virtual goods trading. The virtual goods are also traded externally in entertainment worlds, but currently without consent of the virtual world vendors[13].

The second thing is the new approach SL took on the content and character layer. In contrast to EU, which covers both layers (b.2) implementing a closed business virtual world, very similar to existing entertainment virtual worlds, SL innovates (b.4 and b.5) by embracing Web 2.0 philosophy and deconstructs the value-chain further, thereby creating new markets. This approach is new and opens business opportunities also for non-entertainment companies.

Conclusion: Recapitulating, different segments offer different opportunities:

---

[12]Entertainment and community virtual worlds also partner with financial institutions, but only for billing purposes. For business virtual worlds this is an integral part of the virtual world itself, not only an implementation of the billing function.

[13]SOE is a noteworthy exception, because it has introduced an own marketplace for virtual goods exchange in 2005 (Sony Online Entertainment 2007).

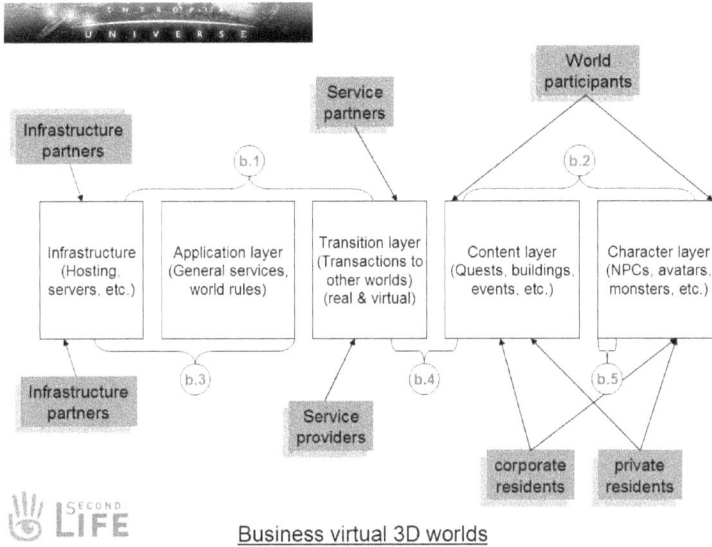

Figure 3.8: Value-chain based comparison of EU against SL

- The **entertainment segment** offers the most intense and immersive virtual worlds. Most virtual worlds are closed or restricted, which makes it easier to sustain a high level of in-world consistency, an important aspect of the immersion factor. This means that business opportunities are few, although they exist. IBM identified the opportunity, entertainment virtual worlds represent for leadership lessons (DeMarco et al. 2007; IBM 2007b).

- The **community segment** offer more business opportunities, as community virtual worlds are usually less restricted than entertainment virtual worlds. In the case of AW, each world can be consistent to increase immersion, but different worlds can be totally different. Here business opportunities come in the form of a virtual meeting place for employees, or as another distribution channel for e-learning. Companies buying worlds can define all things necessary to create an environment for their needs. The world participants have few or no rights to change anything. This is best compared to normal publishing web applications.

- The **business segment** offers most business opportunities. Unrestricted virtual worlds like SL have also a low immersion factor. In SL a medieval castle can be build right beside an oil rig. A resident can take a walk in his shiny knight's armor through a futuristic town. This is possible, because SL embraces the Web 2.0 philosophy, so every resident is allowed to contribute content. On the other side, companies are free to do about everything. Besides marketing focused activities or education they can also generate virtual revenue with virtual products which can be transformed into real revenue.

3.3.2   Virtual 3D world business models

Based on the preceding analysis three generic business models can be derived:

- **C-business:** Creative business or *c-business*, encompasses activities around the application layer. This includes a complete virtual world, or parts of it by further deconstructing the application layer. C-business is suitable for corporate or business level strategies. On the functional level, i.e. marketing, the cost associated with c-business offset the benefits by far.

- **I-business:** Interconnecting business, or *i-business* encompasses activities around the transition layer, be it transition between the real world and the virtual world or between virtual worlds. I-business is also suitable for corporate or business level strategies only. While companies like IGE have built their corporate value proposition on i-business, financial institutes like Deutsche Bank would just adapt their existing e-business strategy on a business level.

- **V-business:** Virtual business, or *v-business* encompasses activities on the content and character layer level happening within virtual worlds, like advertising, selling virtual goods or offering services in virtual worlds. V-business is suitable for all strategy levels.

These three generic business models are in general independent of the virtual world segments, although certain segments currently promote certain business models. In chapter 4 the three business model forms will be examined and evaluated in more detail, by looking at implementations in and around Second Life.

Chapter 4

Business models in the context of Second Life

In this chapter the business models identified in section 3.3 are evaluated by continuing the segmentation analysis started in section 3.2. In each section two business model variants are described. Then, one case is presented implementing one business model variant. After analyzing the according segment attractiveness, using *Porter's 5-Forces*[1], the case is evaluated by examining the implementation of the pertaining key success factors and the segment scope selection observed.

Linden Lab with Second Life was used as c-business case study in section 4.1. ACS[2] with its *AnsheX* service was used as i-business case study in section 4.2. The IBM HR department with its related v-business activities in Second Life was used as v-business case study in section 4.3.

4.1 Creative business models

4.1.1 C-business model variants

Creating virtual 3D worlds: A company interested in creating virtual worlds has to decide in which virtual world segment to compete. According to figure 3.4 it has to decide on three segmentation variables:

1. *Customer group focus.* The interviews conducted showed that players would

---

[1]A brief introduction to this methodology can be found in appendix A.4.
[2]Anshe Chung Studios

probably not enter a business virtual world, but seek out entertainment virtual worlds instead. On the other side, business people seldom have the time needed to enter entertainment virtual worlds.

2. *Virtual world openness.* Unrestricted worlds are fully compatible for B2C and B2B business, while closed worlds further predominantly B2C business.

3. *Virtual world theme.* It can be a fixed theme, like *fantasy, science fiction* or *superheroes.* It could also be *present day* based with themed areas, like theme parks in the real world.

As depicted in figure 3.4, all virtual world vendors examined took this approach.

Creating service layers of virtual 3D worlds: By further deconstructing the *application layer* value-chain link, as depicted in figure 4.1, more business opportunities can be found through vertical segmentation. There is no reason, why specialist companies should not leverage their core competence and offer single services of the application layer implementing the *layer player* strategy described by Heuskel (1999, pp. 58-61). This form of c-business seems more high-risk at

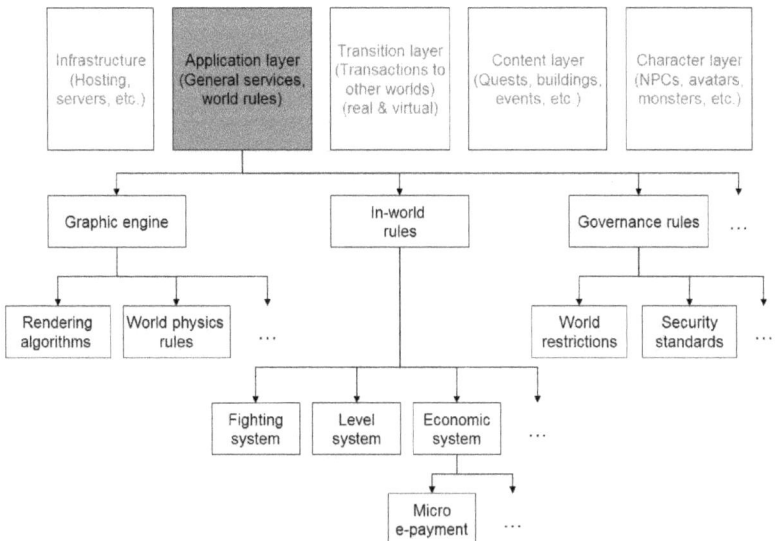

Figure 4.1: Deconstruction of value-chain application layer

the first glance, considering that key success factors and differentiation of virtual worlds depend on the quality and combination of the application layer aspects as a whole. From a strict business perspective, this was also the case in other industries, like telecommunication or automotive, before companies started value-chain deconstruction. C-business in this form would allow the formation of virtual companies for the duration of the virtual world life-cycle, mitigating the investment risk by distributing it and increasing the quality by focusing on core competencies (cp. Fink and Knoblach 2003, pp. 191-195). This would enable a high investment closed entertainment segment quality level for all segments, as well as further open standards in virtual worlds, a prerequisite for wide adoption of virtual worlds, according to Thorsten Seelowe.

4.1.2 World creation – Second Life by Linden Lab

With the introduction of SL in 2003, Linden Lab had to face existing competitors in the form of community virtual world providers like Activeworlds. They targeted similar customer groups with similar offerings, like hosting servers and providing application layer services (compare figure 3.7). In the same year, MindArk released EU as a closed business virtual world in a science fiction setting, emphasizing transition layer business opportunities. To differentiate from existing and emerging virtual worlds, LL pursued appropriate value-chain deconstruction approaches to gain competitive advantages in new segments: They targeted the unrestricted business virtual world segment, avoiding its competitors (step 1 in figure 4.2). Facing scarce resources and capabilities in the beginning, LL pursued the *orchestrator* strategy described by Heuskel (1999, pp. 65-68), in that it partnered up on the transition layer with virtual exchange specialist GOM[3]. Two years later the situation changed and LL changed its strategy to that of an *integrator*, reconstructing the value-chain and driving GOM out of this market[4] by realizing a currency exchange service by themselves (Combs 2005). Today, the website of SL does not even refer to any third party offering exchange service anymore (see Linden Research Inc. 2007c) and an Internet search revealed almost

---

[3]Gaming Open Market
[4]and out of business, as GOM focused its resources and capabilities solely on SL disregarding other virtual worlds, in contrast to IGE, which still does business with MMORPG virtual goods.

all major virtual goods exchange platforms basically ignore SL as virtual world. Ebay offerings are disregarded here, as they lack the transaction security guarantee given by companies like IGE or LL.

LL also pursued a *market maker* strategy with their value-chain deconstruction of

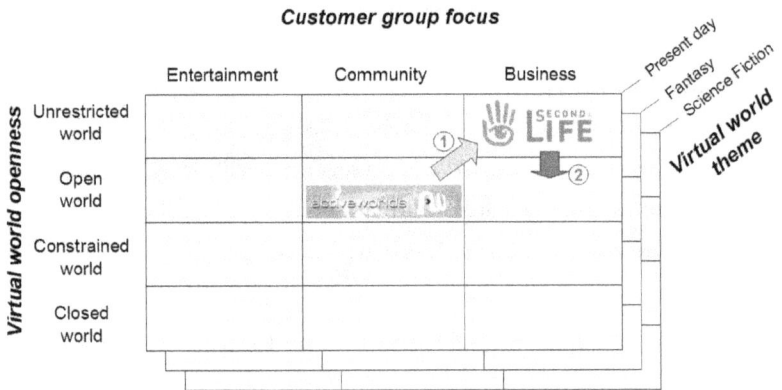

Figure 4.2: C-business model and applied segment strategy of Linden Lab

the *content* and *character layer*, leveraging the Web 2.0 approach to a much higher extent than comparable competitors, like Activeworlds or MindArk. The new market they introduced was the ability to design and construct virtual things within SL, while keeping the IP rights. This and the massive marketing activities leaded to the hype, which can be observed today.

The target group of SL is not restricted to individuals or corporations. Nevertheless, looking at the discussion on the Internet and taking into accounts the interview with Arc, it becomes clear that *players* are not a target group of SL, as the world lacks direction or a goal.

4.1.3   Attractiveness of business virtual world segment

Threat of new entrants: The threat of new entrants differs according to the entrant origin. Competitors from other virtual world segments can leverage most of their knowledge to enter the discussed segment. For example companies like Blizzard or SOE have enough capital, skills, technology capabilities and a strong brand to enter. Therefore the barriers to mobility are rather low.

Examples for potential new entrants from outside the industry are media companies, which further the exploit of reality TV show concepts like *Big Brother* or *Playboy Mansion*. ISP[5]s could leverage their experience with Internet provision to enter this market as well. Another type of entrants could come from industry joint ventures, with industry-specific in-world physics needs[6].

For c-business there are no significant **economies of scale** effects[7], as there is no physical input resource needed to develop a virtual world. **Brand differentiation** on the other side is a strong entry barrier. The business virtual world segment requires a strong security and trust reputation on the vendor side, because business virtual worlds include real financial transactions. Also a strong brand suggests a successful world which implies more potential customers and future-proof investment possibilities mitigating the risks of proprietary technologies currently in use. LL further increased this barrier with their marketing activities around SL. The SL brand can be considered very strong, although a recent Internet survey among specialists and management in the Internet industry shows that more than 50% consider SL an overrated hype (novomind AG 2007, p. 6). Although the **capital requirements** for world creating c-business lie between $5-30 million, depending on the type and quality of virtual worlds (Castronova 2005, p. 128), the SL case demonstrated that an incremental approach is feasible for the unrestricted business virtual world segment, as competition intensity is still low. **Skilled resources** can pose a significant barrier of entry. Virtual worlds emerged only recently out of the entertainment industry as a whole, which makes it difficult to find enough appropriate skills to satisfy the growing demand. **Technological prerequisites** also represent a high entry barrier, because virtual worlds are technologically demanding highly parallel systems. Additional security and availability requirements particular for the discussed segment further increase this barrier of entry. Maintaining the running virtual world also increases the demand on good maintenance processes like hot fixes (also called *patches*) or up-

---

[5]Internet Service Provider

[6]For example the textile industry could leverage algorithms, which let virtual fabric behave like real fabric, so that people could try clothes remote and buy them online (for algorithm see Scholz and Magnor 2006).

[7]C-business does not include application hosting or product distribution, where economies of scale do matter. For application hosting, server space or CPU cycle time are lowered with on demand offerings, through which the company is charged per time and space *used* and not per time and space *purchased.*

dates. Taking all this into consideration, the threat of entry from outside the virtual world industry can be considered low, whereas the threat of entries from other segments is significant.

Rivalry among existing firms: Tower Group estimated a 36.5% compound annual **industry growth rate** in MMORPG participation, which is higher than the 20.1% increase of the general Internet population from 2000 to 2005. They consider virtual worlds as an emerging market and predict it to "grow to 40 million people spending $9 billion annually by 2010" (Nelsetuen 2006). The $9 billion are revenue derived primarily through direct monthly subscription fees. Other sources claim a similar market growth (see James et al. 2004, pp. 10-14). Castronova on the other side agrees that the market is growing, but also points out that the supply of virtual worlds grows even more, which adds to the competitive pressure on the virtual world industry (Castronova 2005, pp. 131-135). Regarding the **number of equal competitors** the business segment and the whole virtual world industry do not differ much. A handful of major competitors compete with multitude small start-ups. This can lead to higher competition in all segments, as few big companies increase rivalry, while unknown start-ups with unknown financial resources and capabilities are difficult to cope with in. According to Castronova the current situation is not that competitive though, because "new worlds tend to target different segments and [...] add their population to the market rather than take users away [...]" (Castronova 2005, p. 139). **Product differentiation** within the business virtual world segment is still high, considering the virtual world theme and the virtual world openness. In this segment the technology plays also an important role in product differentiation. If new virtual worlds are similar in all aspects to an existing virtual world, they will fail, because switching cost of buyers are quite high. If technological standards are established, the product differentiation will erode to a certain degree, since investments can be carried over to a new virtual world. The industry **exit barriers** are high. Virtual worlds need specialized skills, like *3D design* or *programming for massively concurrent environments* skills not easily redeployed to other e-business activities. The segment exit barriers for virtual world companies active in other segments are low, as they can reuse a significant portion of their resources and capabilities. Taking all this into consideration, the rivalry among existing firms within the business segment can be considered low but this could easily change with new entries from other segments.

Threat of substitute products or services: There are differences between substitutes from other segments and substitutes from outside the virtual world industry. Substitutes from outside the industry include, among others, Web 2.0 based collaboration solutions and different, more effective marketing channels.

The **relative price performance of substitutes** is more significant for corporate than for private consumers. Corporate consumers normally want to solve business problems. If the added value a virtual 3D world solution offers is not leveraged, it can be easily substituted with a reasonably priced Internet solution. Considering substitutes from other segments, **short technological innovation cycles** pose a significant threat. Virtual worlds with newer technologies adapted to the new graphical hardware capabilities and the currently available broadband bandwidth, are more attractive than older worlds. For example the streaming technology SL is build upon was perfect for low network bandwidth, but increasingly annoying, if enough bandwidth is available, according to multiple interview partners. Old virtual worlds do not end to exist immediately, but their population is reduced to the hard-core population reducing also profits and v-business attractiveness. For private consumers the **perceived level of product differentiation** is high. For virtual worlds it is defined along the segmentation variables introduced in section 2.2.2. For corporate consumers the level of differentiation is low. Much of the offerings could be done with Web 2.0 technologies. For example, applications like Microsoft's *MSN Virtual Earth* or Google's *Google Earth* are a significant threat to SL's advertising related value proposition, as they are based on the real world after all (Jones 2006). Joe Triskaidekaphobia brings it to the point by demanding corporate consumers to "change mindset – [to] not copy what you have done in 2D to 3D". Taking all this into consideration, the threat of substitution for the business segment can be considered high from other segments as well as from other web-based e-business solutions.

Bargaining power of buyers: For the business virtual world segment there are two groups of buyers or consumers: private and corporate buyers. The bargaining power of private buyers is relatively low, as virtual worlds are **differentiated**. If for example SOE decided to expand the virtual world scope of *Star Wars Galaxies* into the business virtual world segment, every private consumer, who wants to be a *Jedi knight*, has to join this world. Joining SL and building some Jedi avatar would not be the same experience. Corporate buyers face a similar situation. Although the value propositions of business virtual worlds are basically **undifferentiated**, SL is currently the only one with a broad value proposition mix and a high awareness level, giving LL a temporary monopoly position within the unconstrained business virtual world segment. For corporate and private consumers **switching cost** are high in virtual worlds, as proprietary technology makes it very difficult to transfer time or money invested from on virtual world to the next. Before entering a virtual world the **price sensitivity** of buyers is rather high. Private buyers evaluate the entertainment factor of the virtual world and the price demanded by the vendor. As this is crucial in the beginning, many vendors offer either time-restricted trial memberships or content-restricted memberships, like the free SL membership, where the resident is not allowed to own land. After entering the virtual world the price sensitivity may erode over time. Corporate buyers evaluate the price against substitution solutions. The price evaluation is supported by high **buyer's information availability** through channels like the Internet, magazines, friends or technology and business consultants in the case of corporate buyers. For corporations, the information available is lower than for private buyers, as the business virtual world segment is not mature yet and there are still few success stories available. The **threat of backward integration** is currently low, as buyers are still testing virtual 3D world possibilities. The risks of backward integration currently outweigh the benefits of using existing virtual worlds. Taking all this into consideration, the bargaining power of buyers can be considered low in the business virtual world segment, mainly because of switching cost and product differentiation.

Bargaining power of suppliers: In the discussed context of c-business there are two major types of suppliers: the infrastructure companies providing application hosting services and the creative development team or persons designing the virtual world.

The relative bargaining power of infrastructure suppliers is somewhat higher than that of virtual world companies. The **supplier switching cost** of an infrastructure company can be considered lower than that the switching cost of the virtual world vendor, although virtual worlds do require high-end hardware. For huge virtual worlds like WoW this ratio is more balanced, as there are few e-business applications needing such volumes in concurrent real-time access. As there are not much reliable application service providers suitable for virtual worlds hosting on the market, their bargaining position is strong. It is offset to some extent by the ability of the virtual world company to also do the hosting thereby **substituting the input**. The **threat of forward integration** is not high from infrastructure suppliers. Although some of them have the technical capability and resources to develop own virtual worlds, they would just create another world, rather than building the same virtual world again.

The relative bargaining power of development teams is generally lower than that of the virtual world company. The **switching cost** of the development team is low compared to the vendor, although there are generally enough programmers available in low-cost countries like India or China. As mentioned above, it is a question of needed skills rather than available time. **Information** about current virtual world developments of competitors is freely available, so that switching options can be acquired easily. Additional information can be obtained through collaboration platforms between peers. **Supplier concentration** is low in regard to development teams, as the concept of a *labor union* is still strange to most of the developers. The **threat of forward integration** by development teams is generally low, although it could happen. Virtual world firms can mitigate this risk by committing key developers to the firm through adequate financial compensations or similar human resource instruments. Taking all this into consideration, the bargaining power of suppliers can be considered high for both, development teams and infrastructure suppliers, because of proprietary technology and the relative lower switching cost of the suppliers.

Conclusion: The segment attractiveness is, according to the preceding industry analysis, rather moderate. Threats of new entries from other segments and the associated potential increase in rivalry within the business virtual world segment make this segment a future challenge. Buyer bargaining power is low while supplier bargaining power is somewhat strong. The high threat of substitution from Web 2.0 applications can be attributed to the huge number of uninspired implementations within virtual worlds. Here c-business companies should actively think about how their customers could leverage the virtual 3D world potential without giving marketing messages at the same time. Taking the results from section 3.1 also into consideration there are opportunities in technological and social changes, but some legal threats for c-business.

Doing c-business in the business virtual world segment is definitely a big opportunity for existing virtual world companies in other segments, as they can easily enter the segment due to their existing resources and capabilities. Companies outside the virtual world industry, like media companies, will face a much higher risk, when entering c-business. Alternatively they could think of partnerships with existing firms.

4.1.4   Evaluation of the c-business model implementation

Linden Lab entered the business virtual world segment at the right time and can now exert first mover advantages in the unrestricted business virtual world segment. How good this was done was assessed by analyzing compliance with the relevant general key success factors identified in section 2.1.3 and 2.2.3 and the relevant in-world key success factors identified in section 3.2.2.

General key success factor compliance: Integrating e-business into the overall strategy is definitely a strength of Linden Lab. The media strategy of Philip Rosedale has so far tremendously furthered the success of SL beyond its technological capabilities. SL is also an **innovative software concept**, as it is the first unrestricted virtual world. This innovation was decisive to circumvent the need for **suitable e-business** and **art skills**, in the order of magnitude needed for MMORPGs.

The diminishing **trust of customers** and **reputation loss** of LL in the last few months can be attributed to unresolved ownership disputes, general hype backlash and decisions taken based on headquarter location. The LL headquarter location within the US can be considered a competitive disadvantage in international markets. Indicators for this trend can be observed in the *SL-and-gambling* discussions as well as in the lost bid for creating a cash-based virtual economy for China which was won by Sweden-based MindArk (Heng 2007). The **low quality, reliability and usability** as well as the **poor performance** of SL are additional weaknesses resulting from the old streaming technology used for SL. Another weakness is the capacity restriction of 40 residents per island, which make big corporate conventions or concerts impossible as Thorsten Seelowe pointed out[8].

In-world key success factor compliance: The only strength of LL is the degree of **freedom and creativity** it provides its residents through SL. The **virtual community management** seems to be low cost, rather than high quality. LL decided to provide concise support only to subscribing residents, which account to only 1.2% of the total residents, based on the June figures noted on page 33. The other residents are advised to use FAQ[9] lists and user forums as information sources. The impact of the virtual community is high, as was shown on page 50, so it is questionable, if this solution is sufficient.

One important weakness lies in the **low immersion factor** observed in SL, as well as in the awkward user interface, a key determinant for **flow experience**. The interviewed SL residents unanimously stated that they felt no immersion in SL, even though some of them experienced immersion with games. Joe for example, although he currently spends 40 days per week in SL, would leave SL without second thought, if it would not be project related. It can also be assumed that the **level of privacy and in-world security systems** is mediocre at best and thereby also a weakness. Indicators for this are for example IBM regulations, which pro-

---

[8]In this regard the author encountered many biased or half-truth number of participants comparisons with WoW during his research. On was the scalability mentioned by Thorsten. The other was the total residents count, where LL count every named avatar, regardless if two of them belong to one person. The adjusted user count is about 35% lower than the advertized one (cp. Linden Research Inc. 2007a, website data with key metrics in excel format). For comparison if Blizzard would count that way, the could at least add another 40 million avatars to their head count.

[9]Frequently Asked Questions

hibit talking about confidential subjects within SL, even if both employees are on IBM islands. Another example is the law suit already described on page 36.

Segment scope selection assessment: LL currently pursues a narrow segment focus strategy. This can be attributed to scarce resources available. If the key success factor compliance is taken into account, this strategy is positive. LL has probably neither the resources nor the capabilities needed to expand into other segments at this point in time. Looking at the low in-world key success factor compliance it is questionable if SL will stay a success story when the media hype is over or when other virtual world companies decide to enter this segment. Joe Triskaidekaphobia sums it up in the following way: "I tend to believe that Second Life might be for 3D-world what Mosaic was for the 2D-world."

4.2   Interconnecting business models

4.2.1   I-business model variants

Interconnecting virtual worlds: This i-business model is about technically interconnecting virtual worlds through standardized protocols and interfaces to make it possible for a user to walk seamlessly between worlds, as Loxagon[10] dreams of. For example users could move from SL to AW to chat with friends. Then in the evening they could meet in WoW to storm *Undercity*. Today they have to log separately into each virtual world to check, if anyone is online in this particular world in the first place.

The reason this is currently not possible at this level is proprietary technology and missing virtual world standards, like higher network protocol layer standards or basic graphical rendering standards, so that object information could be visualized in different virtual world specific ways. Also virtual world vendors would lose a significant portion of their current bargaining power. If open standards are agreed upon in the future, as Thorsten Seelowe asks for, virtual worlds could become connected to form an **Interworld**, analogue to the Internet evolution described in section 1.1.

---

[10]The complete interview with Loxagon can be found in appendix B.4.

On a lower level, potential business opportunities with i-business can be observed within virtual worlds, which are actually more like virtual universes. For example WoW, like nearly all MMORPGs, is divided into many virtual world instances. Blizzard transfers avatars between realms or accounts for a fee of 19.99 €. Other MMORPGs take also a fee for transfers. In AW or SL, users can move free of charge between different worlds or islands[11] respectively. The reason behind this difference is the technical maximum user restriction, which is in AW and SL rather small, as was noted in the interviews (see appendix B.5 and B.6).

Other noteworthy opportunities for first movers, beside avatar or virtual goods transfer, would be the development of unified development environments for multiple virtual worlds. Such services would decrease the exit barriers for buyers as well as virtual world vendors.

Intermediating between worlds: Intermediation between worlds is currently done by companies like *IGE, ACS* or *Team VIP*. The intermediation takes place either between the real world and virtual worlds or (in)directly between virtual worlds. Virtual items transferred span from virtual currency to avatars. A company interested in i-business has to decide on three key points:

- *Virtual worlds:* Which virtual worlds are in scope?

- *Scope of intermediation:* What virtual goods are to be intermediated, only currency or the full spectrum?

- *Quality of services:* What kind of services is offered concerning the transactions? Secure transactions or basic services like Ebay?

All companies examined diversified over different virtual worlds while choosing different scope of intermediation and quality of service.

4.2.2   Exchanging Linden Dollars – AnsheX by ACS

ACS Ltd. was founded in China by Ailin and Guntram Graef in January 2006, after a period of v-business model testing in Germany since June 2004. The company has, as of April 2007, 60 full time employees (ACS Ltd. 2007b). Ailin Graef,

---

[11]Islands cannot be reached by flying or swimming!

also known as *Anshe Chung* started her SL v-business success story in SL with an investment of only $9.95. After earning enough seed money with virtual escort services, she entered the v-business of selling avatar related products, as well as virtual property development and trading (Hutcheon 2007).

ACS offers services on the *character*, *content* and the *transition layer* of the virtual world value-chain, as can be seen in figure 4.3. They are active in SL, IMVU and EU, where ACS recently acquired a banking license (Wallace 2007a). There was also one reference to ACS involvement in the virtual world *There*, but this could not be confirmed through other sources.

According to company information the projected revenue for 2007 is estimated

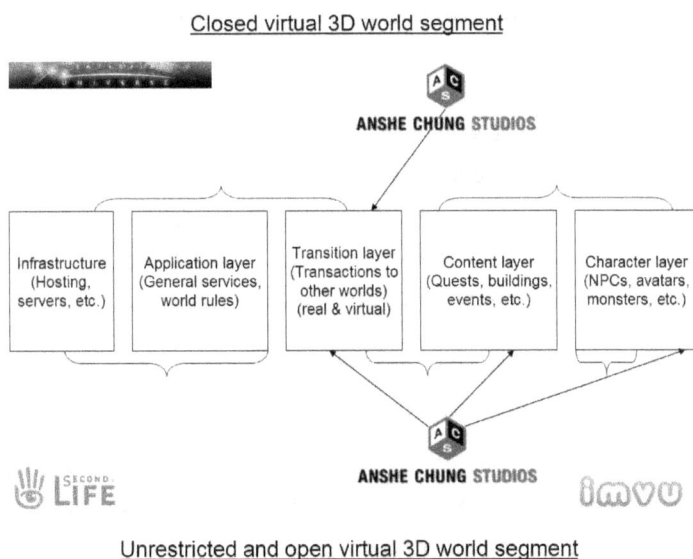

Figure 4.3: Value-chain strategy of ACS Ltd.

to L$1.5 billion, which translate to about $5.6 million. Revenue in SL contributes 80% of the total revenue, while the rest is generated with other virtual worlds (ACS Ltd. 2007b). All facts are stated in virtual currency and are thereby subject to similar forces comparable to those applying to unrealized capital gains on spot markets, with the difference that virtual worlds are controlled by just one unregulated company.

To cope with this significant risk, ACS tries to diversify to multiple virtual

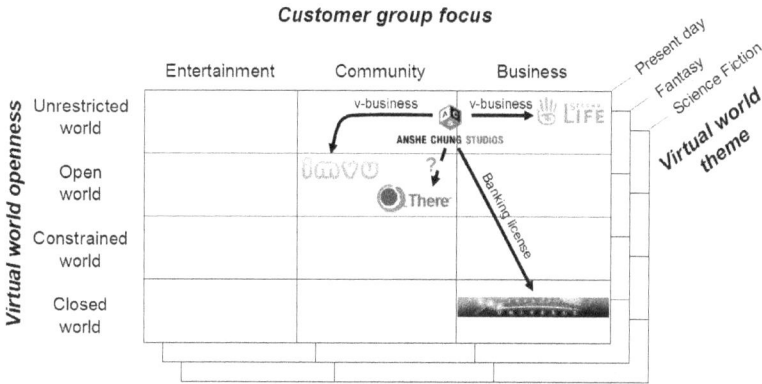

Figure 4.4: Diversification strategy of ACS Ltd.

worlds, as can be seen in figure 4.4. This strategy has proved to be successful, as can be seen at the examples of *IGE* and *Team VIP* in comparison to *GOM*, which focused on SL alone and was driven out of business by LL, as mentioned on page 57. In IMVU, ACS offers the same breadth of services as in SL, while in EU it is confined to offering only currency exchange.

The currency exchange system of ACS is called *AnsheX* and is, according to company information, "the largest virtual currency exchange for IMVU and the second largest exchange for Second Life currency"(ACS Ltd. 2007a). Additionally to this, ACS also announced a virtual-currency-only *inter-world financial market* to provide its customer with an opportunity to diversify their assets over multiple virtual worlds to mitigate investment risk (ACS Ltd. 2007a; Wallace 2007b).

4.2.3 Attractiveness of currency exchange in SL

Threat of new entrants: Potential new entrants to currency exchange could be start-ups, financial institutions, competitors from other virtual worlds or the virtual world vendor. Currency exchange needs trust and secure transactions. Because of this **brand differentiation** and the **technological prerequisites** required are high. **Capital requirements** should be high, but they are not in fact. Aside from the capital needed to set up the exchange platform, there is capital needed to build up reserves to cover exchange transactions. Currently all competitors within SL and other virtual worlds lack the capital needed in this regard.

The platform is usually a normal e-commerce application with back-end connections into the virtual world and to financial systems for the financial transaction of the real currency. Because of this, the barrier of **skilled resources** is not higher than for other e-business solutions. Generally the threat of new entrants from outside the segment of currency trading is low. Since the barriers to mobility for existing currency trading companies, as well as for virtual world vendors are low, the overall threat of new entries is high.

Rivalry among existing firms: Rivals of ACS Ltd. are Linden Lab and Europe-based *Eldex*, which specialized in exchanging L$ for €. The entry of LL into this business severely increased competition and already put *GOM* out of business. So in terms of **number of equal competitors**, SL is a monopoly of LL with small competitors. **Product differentiation** is also low. With the entry of LL the margins accruing from buy-sell-rate differences have fallen to about 17% compared to the buy rates offered by LL. This may seem high, but is much lower, than the difference charged in the competitive exchange market of IMVU. The difference found in AnsheX for example is around 40%. The **industry growth rate** of currency exchange is rapidly growing, since overall virtual economy grows also, as described on page 41. The **exit barriers** can be high, depending on the virtual currency available at the point of exit. Large volumes of virtual currency are currently not convertible into real currency without disturbing the overall economy. Additionally, exchange service providers can decline requests, based on market situation or real currency coverage. Overall the rivalry and competitive pressure in SL is high, whereas in other virtual worlds it is lower.

Threat of substitute products or services: Ebay can be regarded as substitute service, since it is just a platform for insecure peer-to-peer transactions, in that Ebay cannot be held liable in the case of fraud. From buyer perspective, the **relative price performance** of Ebay in terms of fees is comparable to the secured transactions offered by AnsheX and LL. It can be offset by peers by offering to exchange large amounts of virtual currency. The **perceived level of service differentiation** is high, because fraud is easier within Ebay. This perception can be mitigated by peers through a high reputation in the Ebay reputation system. If buyer trust can be established, the peer gets a full fledged trading platform on demand, which renders investment in the development and maintenance of e-business solutions needless. From supplier perspective this would increase the **relative price performance** of Ebay. Overall the threat of substitutes is rather low.

Bargaining power of buyers: As the services compared are secure transactions, the **product is undifferentiated** and the **switching cost** of the buyer from LL to AnsheX or some other secure transaction provider is low. To cope with the **price sensitivity** of the buyer, competitors to LL try to offer better service in terms of transaction speed and reliability. Whether it is better, could not be assessed without exchanging high volumes of currency. The **buyer's information availability** is, as with all Internet based services, rather high. Competitors try to diffuse information, by stating different rates. For example, LL offers a buy rate for L$ of $1 : L$265, subject to the market rate. AnsheX offers L$10,000 for $39.99. To be comparable, this first has to be translated by the buyer into an exchange rate of around $1 : L$250 to discover that it is about 6% less, than the buyer would get from LL directly. The **threat of backward integration** by buyers is possible, in that they trade directly without any intermediating party, but it comes at the cost of transaction security loss. Overall the relative bargaining power of buyers is high in SL.

Bargaining power of suppliers: The suppliers to services like AnsheX are the virtual world companies. In the example of SL it is LL. The **threat of forward integration** happened already, as mentioned before. The relative bargaining power of ACS is lower than that of the supplier. ACS still does 80% of its revenue with SL, so the **switching cost** is higher than that of LL. The difference is currently not so high, as it could be, because ACS is *the success story* of Second Life and one of LL biggest customers. There were actually some rumors of ACS thinking about **substituting the input** with an own currency called *Anshe$* but this idea is somewhat unrealistic, as long as LL has full control over its world. Also the rumor source could be the SL April's Fool joke of 2006 (Jonas and Spaight 2006). ACS could of course build up its own virtual world, but the author strongly doubts that they have the resources or capabilities to do this (yet). Finally LL does have all **information available** regarding financial transactions within SL, whereas ACS does only have published information about the virtual economy of SL. Overall the relative bargaining power of LL is high.

Conclusion: The transition layer market for currency exchange within SL is not attractive anymore, since the threat of entry is low, while the relative buyer and supplier bargaining power are high. When LL entered this virtual industry, it transformed into a monopoly of LL, leaving little room for other competitors. Substitution threat of currency exchange is not high, as it is a basic service.

A segment specific opportunity is the ability of service providers, like ACS or LL, to prolong the currency exchange service process, to realize interest profits. It is the same mechanism financial institutes are using, when executing bank transfers of consumers. The difference here is that in virtual worlds this could take several days or even weeks, whereas in real life this process takes one to three days in general. Taking also the macro environmental factors into account, the attractiveness does not increase. The only opportunity of interest is the future growth of virtual world users and thereby the growth of the virtual economy, which promotes continuous business.

4.2.4   Evaluation of the i-business model implementation

ACS emerged from the virtual economy of SL and now tries to diversify to other worlds to mitigate risk and leverage acquired skills. How good this was done with the AnsheX service is assessed by analyzing compliance with the relevant general key success factors identified in section 2.1.3 and 2.2.3 and the relevant in-world key success factors identified in section 3.2.2.

General key success factor compliance: The website of ACS shows that they pursue an **integrated e-business strategy**. The personal stardom of Ailin Graef, better known as *Anshe Chung* is one key value, which ACS hones and grows. The needed *e-business skills* for the Internet-based AnsheX application are available. As it probably handles rather small amounts of data, the **quality, reliability and**

usability of it is sufficient[12].

The evaluation of the degree of **customer trust and reputation** is ambivalent. ACS should be able to translate the high product design quality as well as Ailin Graef's personal publicity into high reputation and customer trust. Individual Internet resources suggest that she is *unscrupulous* and *greedy*. Although it cannot be determined, if the majority thinks this way, or just some jealous residents, it is definitely a risk, which must be addressed through proper public relation.

In-world key success factor compliance: There are only two of the five in-world key success factors relevant for the AnsheX service. The first is **transaction security**, which is expected to be on a sufficiently high level, since not one resource could be found, claiming the opposite. The second success factor is the **virtual community management**. As described above, the community management seems to be a current weakness of ACS. The issues do not come from dissatisfaction with the AnsheX service, but from the overall public behavior of ACS in the virtual worlds, they operate. ACS has become a profit oriented company, grown out of a playful virtual community. Rising tensions should be foreseeable and proactive handled, because the customer base is still the same virtual community.

Segment scope selection assessment: ACS recognized the threat of operating in only one virtual world. They implemented a broad diversification strategy over multiple virtual worlds and in multiple segments, as was shown in figure 4.4. As their home market is SL, it still generates the biggest revenue stream with 80% of total revenue. The recent acquisition of a banking licence in the EU virtual world could prove an excellent investment, since MindArk had won the Chinese bid to create a cash-based virtual economy Heng (2007). As ACS is based in China, it is a big opportunity. The overall strategy by ACS to only do currency exchange business with virtual world explicitly allowing this minimizes the threat of law suits or major issues with virtual world providers, which could prove fatal to overall business.

---

[12]The author assumes that the revenue stream from AnsheX is small compared to the overall revenue stream of ACS, and therefore the transaction volume processed is also small.

4.3   Virtual business models

V-business possibilities are *virtually* limitless, because each virtual world is an economic space on its own. It can be *conceptually* compared to different national markets, where each virtual world resembles one national market. As in the real world, certain strategies and actions are available in order to enter a new national market. A discussion of all these possibilities would take too much space and is therefore omitted. In order to narrow the scope of the thesis, the possibilities are classified according to figure 4.5. V-business models, utilizing virtual worlds only as additional advertisement channel, will not be discussed further.

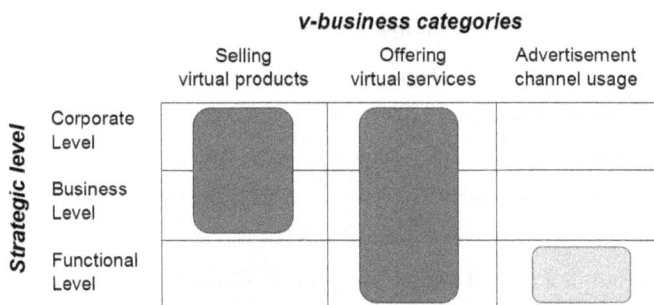

Figure 4.5: Applicability of v-business categories to strategic levels.

4.3.1   V-business model variants

Selling virtual products: Selling virtual products in Second Life for *real money* (indirectly) is probably the most astonishing v-business model at first glance. Virtual products could be a replica of real products or genuine virtual products. Everything which can be sold in real life, can also be sold in virtual worlds, as buyers are still humans in both scenarios[13]. If a company decides to do this kind of v-business, it has to decide on three key points:

- *Virtual worlds:* As in i-business, one has to decide – which virtual worlds are in scope?

---

[13]This includes also *skins, body modifications* or other *plastic surgery products* at virtually no risk to health. Even modifications toward animal shape are possible also in the real world, though the modification degree is (still) limited.

- *Virtual product group:* What virtual products should be produced? Clothing, cars, houses, etc.

- *V-business strategy:* The e-business strategy approach described by Wirtz encompasses *strategic objective definition, situation analysis, strategy formulation* and *strategy implementation* (Wirtz 2001, pp. 148-150). It is modified into a v-business strategy approach by focusing on the virtual world as an external environment[14].

Companies must be aware of the threats coming from the high bargaining power of buyers, a high substitution risk and low entry barriers. Market analysis is critical, as not all industries or segments are saturated yet. Additionally the exit barriers are rather low, because all virtual products must be *designed* with a similar set of development tools. So if a company exits woman dress wear to enter car design the only loss would be specialized *clothing design* skills.

Offering virtual services: Offering virtual services can take any form, from virtual event management to lectures, advertisement campaigns or news services. In unconstrained virtual worlds like SL, even writing *quests* is possible. The main question a company must consider is whether any virtual infrastructure is needed at all? For example is it necessary in SL to have their own virtual hall or their own island for events, lectures or concerts? IBM and Harvard law school for example have chosen to own island and meeting places in SL[15].

The possibilities discussed so far are examples for corporate or business level v-business. If a company wants to integrate v-business as part of its overall e-business strategy on a functional level, it has to think about three key points:

- *Virtual worlds:* Which virtual worlds are in scope?

- *Virtual world leverage:* How can the unique possibilities of the particular virtual world segment be leveraged?

- *Seamless e-business integration:* V-business solutions must be integrated into the overall e-business strategy to reach high user acceptance.

---

[14]That means, the virtual world becomes the macro environment and the in-world virtual industry becomes the micro environment.

[15]Within SL the reader can search for *IBM* to teleport to the IBM facilities or search for *Brenkman* to teleport to the Harvard law school facilities.

4.3.2   Human resource activities in Second Life – IBM HR

IBM has embraced social networking with Web 2.0 technologies and also integrated virtual worlds seamlessly into its internal e-business strategy (Bulkeley
2007). SL is currently the main focus of IBM, which owns over 50 islands. Those
islands represent the base for internal, as well as client focused virtual world activities. Beside SL, IBM is also active in *PlaneShift* and researches the value propositions to business of entertainment worlds, like *WoW*.

The HR department of IBM "spent more than $700 million training its workforce,
with employees spending more than 18 million hours – or 55.5 hours per employee – on training" in 2005 (Friedman 2006). IBM's main challenges in HR
lie in the company size, the global distribution of its employees and its human
resource growth rates in emerging markets like India and China (Kutik 2007).
To be able to provide the same customer facing quality of service globally, IBM
established a strong corporate culture, which complements the high technological and consulting skills of its employees worldwide. To increase efficiency and
effectiveness in teaching this corporate culture, as well as other skills to its employees, IBM HR leverages the unique possibilities given by virtual worlds with
four e-learning initiatives:

- **IBM@play** is a program intended to socialize new hires in India to the IBM
  corporate culture and to address the rapid and distributed hiring, according
  to Chuck Hamilton, Learning Solutions Leader of IBM's *Center for Advanced
  Learning* (Kutik 2007). In the overall e-business strategy deployed by IBM
  HR this program provides employees with another channel for e-learning
  (Friedman 2006).

- **Fresh Blue** is a program intended for interns in China, who plan to join
  IBM after graduation. Interns in China are not employees and therefore
  have no access to the IBM network. With *Fresh Blue* they can meet remotely
  and "learn tasks ranging from doing expense reports to interacting with
  clients" (Kutik 2007). With this approach, IBM hopes new employees will
  be productive much sooner (Friedman 2006).

- **Sales Quest** is another program deployed in China, which provides full sales training to new salespeople. In Chinese culture relationship-building is critical. The virtual world environment of *Sales Quest* helps to take this cultural specialty into account. Salespeople can build relationships with other employees, while learning sales techniques and competing for prizes (Friedman 2006; Kutik 2007).

- **Greater IBM** is primarily focused on the U.S., where IBMers, retirees and those still working, can use SL to "mentor new hires through speed mentoring, group meetings, and more" (Friedman 2006). But *Greater IBM* is more than just about mentoring; it is about the *networking* of people, who were once IBMers, even if they now work for other companies. The SL representation is only part of an overall e-business strategy, also including Web 2.0 platforms like *Xing* and *LinkedIn* (IBM 2007c). Since April 2007 this program has also been implemented to Germany.

4.3.3 Attractiveness of SL for hiring and education

Threat of new entrants: One of the key B2B value propositions of SL is education, as was described in subsection 2.3.3. For companies outside SL, the **capital requirements** to do education in SL are rather low, compared to classrooms or a full-fledged e-business solution, since LL provides a basic infrastructure. For regular operation of non-public education the purchase of a private island is mandatory. To test if SL is the right place to conduct virtual classes, LL offers educators a one semester trial called *Campus: Second Life* to experiment with virtual classes (Linden Research Inc. 2007b). Nevertheless educators or companies still need **skilled resources** to actually build up the virtual infrastructure. On the functional strategy level the **brand differentiation** is currently negligible, as buyers are mostly existing (new) employees or students rather than new customers. This however will change in the future. Overall the threat of new entrants, wanting to use SL for education is high, whereas on a functional level the threat is negligible.

Rivalry among existing firms: The rivals of IBM in SL are other companies, competing for tomorrow's technical top talents. All afore mentioned IBM activities are focused on communicating corporate culture and building up relationships, two strong factors in retaining employees. In this context, the rivalry among existing firms is high. SL is a potential source for competitive advantage: The **number of equal competitors** within SL is comparatively low. Even if another company extends its presence to SL, it will not profit from the SL hype anymore, as the *first mover* wave is over. The **product differentiation** in virtual worlds should be higher than with web-based applications. SL, as unrestricted business virtual world, offers nearly every freedom to design an education lesson, from plain *PowerPoint* presentations up to role-playing business situations or 3D multimedia presentations of technical subjects. The **exit barriers** are not too high: While companies, faced with proprietary technology, cannot easily reuse the technical skills acquired to build up education in SL, they can reuse their new concepts and transfer them to other virtual worlds. Finally, the author assumes that SL in particular is a **magnet for technology top talents**, because of the current media hype. Technology companies, wanting a fair share of the available top talents, have to seek out places where those talents are. As top talents are dispersed globally, it would be too costly to check out every university in real life. Therefore being in SL and trying to hire or educate people can be considered a competitive advantage for technology companies. Overall the rivalry among existing firms, although high in the real world, is still low in SL.

Threat of substitute products or services: Substitutes to SL are other virtual worlds, like AW, Web 2.0 based e-business solutions or traditional HR solutions, like classroom lectures. The **relative price performance of substitutes** is a key determinant for substitute efficiency on a functional level. IBM for example uses SL in situations where the cost for alternative HR solutions is higher. The **price performance** of the SL-based v-business solutions *IBM@play*, *Fresh Blue* and *Sales Quest* is high compared to e-business solutions or traditional HR solutions, because they leverage SL specific benefits, i.e. the graphical interactivity needed to role-play certain situations. The price performance compared to other virtual worlds could be low, because from a cost perspective, other more restricted virtual worlds offer more virtual infrastructure out of the box. SL on the other hand offers unrestricted possibilities of designing the infrastructure required. So with other virtual worlds it is a trade-off between price and solution design.

Solution effectiveness is determined by the **perceived level of product differentiation**. If SL is used, for example to just present *PowerPoint* presentations the
email distribution of the presentation is more effective, as people can view it at
their own pace offline. The technological maximum capacity of SL of 40 residents
per island also plays a significant role. Virtual worlds with a higher capacity can
be considered more effective. Also, **ease of use** is important. *Greater IBM* for example is based on SL and Web 2.0 e-business solutions alike. Logging into *Xing*
or *LinkedIn* is much easier than logging into SL. The only infrastructure needed
is an Internet connection and a web browser. SL on the other hand needs at least
some medium graphic card, Windows or Apple Macintosh operating system, a
broadband connection and a current release of the SL client. Although SL can
differentiate between e-business solutions, its differentiation against other virtual worlds, considering the **short technological innovation cycles**, is rather low.
Overall the threat of substitute solutions to SL is high.

Bargaining power of buyers: In this context the buyers are employees or external top talents[16]. The relative bargaining power of employees, compared to the
employer is comparatively low, since alternative learning solutions are again determined by the employer.
The relative bargaining power of top talents, compared to corporations is high.
Top talents usually have a high degree of **information availability**. Also when
corporations are externally viewed, they are **not differentiated** as employers, because they generally do not describe all tangible and intangible benefits associated with corporate employment, out of competitive considerations[17]. SL is still
one innovative way to approach this target group and increase differentiation
against competition. The **switching cost** of top talents is, like in any e-business solution, higher than that of the corporation. Prospective employees can just choose
to apply directly to another corporation or be convinced by a real life corporate
representative at a normal university company fair, regardless of any SL based

---

[16]For *educators* the buyers would, of course, be real customers. For this discussion this group
is negligible, as their v-business solution would be at least on the business strategy level, rather
than on the functional level.

[17]Quantitative information like exact salary, degree of other financial benefits or the value of
financial security programs are not made public.

contacts.

Bargaining power of suppliers: The suppliers of companies doing education and hiring in SL are LL and island or virtual facilities owners.

The relative bargaining power of LL is rather high. The **information available** to LL is comprehensive concerning amount of people, expected revenue and volume. Also for companies, the **supplier switching cost** is relatively low, as was described previously. While LL could switch easily to another company, a company had to leave SL to switch supplier, thereby experiencing **high exit cost**. If education is deemed a lucrative business by LL, they could also decide to **forward integrate**, like they did with currency exchange service, as described in subsection 4.1.2.

The relative bargaining power of third parties is rather low. The **information available** to third parties is not as comprehensive as that of LL. Additionally the **supplier switching cost** are comparatively higher, depending on the companies resources and capabilities. If the buyer company has technological capabilities the switching cost are higher than with a company without technological capabilities. Nevertheless there is a relative high **supplier concentration**, which in turn increases the switching cost of them, as switching a customer means loosing a customer to competition. Finally the threat of **forward integration** may be high, if adequate resources and capabilities are available, but is compensated with the threat of **backward integration** by buyers, purchasing islands or virtual facilities.

Conclusion: The segment attractiveness is, according to the preceding industry analysis, rather high from a functional strategy level perspective, while moderately high from a business or corporate strategy level perspective: Threat of new entries into SL is high, but for companies using SL as part of their internal HR strategy, the threat is not relevant. As SL is still new and companies currently try to figure out how to use virtual worlds, the low rivalry among existing companies will stay that way for some time. On a functional level it also takes some pressure away from the high rivalry level in the quest for tomorrow's top talents. Buyer bargaining power is low for employees. Top talents have inherently a high bargaining power compared to companies, so SL does not change this fact. Supplier bargaining power is generally rather weak, with the exception of LL. The high threat of substitution from Web 2.0 applications and other virtual worlds can be attributed to the huge number of copied 2D Internet concepts into SL, as well as technical limits within SL.

Also, taking the results from section 3.1 into consideration, there are opportunities in technological and social change, particularly with the critical scenario driver E_1, because this increases the possibility that virtual worlds will be the place where top talents can be found. Also S_5 is in this regard important, since presence awareness and the shared experiences accruing from it are unique features of virtual worlds, which can be leveraged for social competence learning.

Offering virtual learning services is definitely a big opportunity for companies with an overall e-learning strategy, as well as for e-learning providers who could be even more elaborate in their solutions, than single companies. Hiring people in virtual worlds is also a big opportunity. Even if the percentage of top talents does not increase, the cost associated with hiring definitely decreases. For example, companies could organize assessment centers in SL, instead of doing this at some real location for widely dispersed applicants.

4.3.4   Evaluation of the v-business model implementation

IBM standardized its intranet and in the last year introduced a lot of Web 2.0 technology to further enhance its internal communication. In this context the leverage of new technologies like virtual worlds by the HR department fits seamlessly into the overall e-business strategy of IBM. How well this was done can be assessed by analyzing compliance with the general key success factors identified in subsection 2.1.3 and 2.2.3.

General key success factor compliance: Integrating e-business into the overall strategy is the core competence of IBM. The integration of SL goes even deeper than just the four initiatives described. IBMers having a SL avatar can connect their IBM *BluePages*[18] data with their SL avatar data in both directions, so that each employee can easily check the identity of his SL counterpart within the IBM

---

[18] *BluePages* is the internal employee data and authentication system used throughout IBM.

intranet. IBM has the **suitable e-business** and **art skills** as well as significant **management support** to realize and further drive **innovative** virtual world solutions, which leverage the unique possibilities of SL. The v-business solutions show a high degree of **quality, reliability and performance**, but are of course subject to the quality, reliability and performance of the underlying SL platform. IBM's **reputation** further supports the success of those v-business solutions. This and the first-mover strategy applied to SL further boosted IBM's SL presence.

In-world key success factor compliance: All v-business solutions implemented are tools, enabling the world-wide IBM **virtual community** and, with regard to the *Greater IBM*, strengthening private and business networks regardless of whether people still work for IBM. To provide maximum **privacy and security** within SL, IBM HR hosts all relevant activities on private IBM islands, where the company has the highest level of control possible.

Segment scope selection assessment: IBM considers the whole virtual world industry, in order to leverage the unique value propositions of all segments. For example, IBM Research (IBM 2007b) and IBM Institute for Business Value (De-Marco et al. 2007) did explore MMORPGs like WoW, and discovered that leadership skills needed in business can also be observed in *raids*[19]. In this regard, raids could become a future substitute for leadership lectures or assessments, considering S_4 on page 45. From an e-learning perspective, the use of virtual worlds will find its place in the e-business tools deployed by IBM.

For the tools supporting the virtual community, this is not as clear. Employees, whose direct work isn't related to SL, find it very time consuming to access *yet another application*. Although IBM managed to integrate SL into their e-business strategy, the integration of SL as an application into the application landscape is currently not possible to the same degree as observed in Web 2.0 applications. This remains a future challenge IBM has to confront.

---

[19]A *raid* in WoW or other MMORPGs are missions consisting of at least 40 players trying to kill some very difficult NPC, like a dragon, a castle lord or other so called *boss enemies*. A *raid* normally needs strong leadership and tactical skills to be successful.

Chapter 5

Conclusion

The analysis of business models, as the example of Second Life has shown, presents multiple business opportunities to innovative companies in virtual worlds: **C-business** is challenging, since capital requirements are high and competition is strong. A company pursuing c-business needs to choose the right segment to start and has to keep up with technology to sustain success. There are currently no virtual world technology component offerings, although this approach could prove to be the right strategy for the business segment, since it introduces technology standards, making virtual worlds more attractive for business.

I-business is currently all about currency exchange. It is very lucrative for first movers, but also very risky, because the threat of forward integration by vendors is high. Other i-business models, like interconnecting virtual worlds, are currently not realized, although such a service would decrease exit barriers for companies investing into particular worlds and would therefore very attractive.

V-business can be integrated into the overall e-business strategy of a company, although the seamless technological integration is not trivial, since virtual worlds are after all single applications. To be successful, the endeavor into v-business needs companies to innovate and break free from the old 2D application patterns. Inside virtual worlds companies find new markets which can be entered using familiar strategies. Every real world product or service conceivable can be transferred into virtual words at minimal production cost.

At the end of the day, companies should always be aware of the *total investment loss* threat, inherently present in all virtual worlds, due to their *virtual* nature.

Appendix A

Used analysis techniques

A.1   Value-chain framework introduction

The value-chain deconstruction and reconstruction, "that is, identifying value-chain elements and identifying possible ways of integrating information along the chain" (Timmers 2000, p. 31 et sqq.), is a systematic way to identify business models along the value chain. There are three analysis steps to identify business models:

- **Value-chain deconstruction:** Identification of single chain elements d_i.

- **Interaction patterns:** Identification of interaction patterns between actors: $I_j \in \{1 : 1, 1 : n, n : 1, n : m\}$. An actor can be a company, information or a product.

- **Value-chain reconstruction:** Identification of $V(\{d_1\}, \{d_2\})$, the integration of two value-chain elements in the context of an interaction pattern I_j.

Business models are "constructed by combining interaction patterns with value chain integration" (Timmers 2000, p. 34). Timmers uses this approach primarily for value-chains, as defined by Porter[1] (1985). Consecutive value-chains add up to a *value system* or industry value-chain (Porter 1985, pp. 33-36). The framework is applied to the virtual world industry value-chain in section 3.3 in order to identify business models.

---

[1]Porter describes the company value-chain with the five primary elements inbound logistics, operations, outbound logistics, marketing & sales and service and the four supporting elements technology development, procurement, human resource management and corporate infrastructure.

A.2   PEST analysis introduction

PEST analysis is used for the analysis of the macro environment, and takes the
four factors described in table A.1 into account. The objective of a macro environmental analysis is according to Narayanan and Fahey (2000, p. 190) to:

1. Provide understanding of current and potential changes in external environment.

2. Provide critical inputs to strategic management.

3. Facilitate and foster strategic thinking in organizations.

Factor	Description
Political	Including areas such as tax policy, employment laws, en-vironmental regulations, tariffs and political stability
Economic	Including areas such as economic growth, interest rates, exchange rates and inflation rate
Social	Including areas such as cultural aspects in general, popu-lation growth rate, age distribution, and career attitudes
Technological	Including areas such as R&D, technology incentives and the rate of technological change

Table A.1: Macro environmental factors

The thesis approach to macro environmental analysis is based on the general approach described by Narayanan and Fahey (2000, pp. 196-202) and consists of
three analysis steps:

1. **Scanning and monitoring:** Changes, events and trends are identified and
   their evolution is determined.

2. **Projecting:** The future direction of environmental changes are evaluated in
   an impact-uncertainty matrix.

3. **Assessing:** The environmental changes are assessed as opportunities or
   threat within the context of the virtual world industry.

Narayanan and Fahey introduce the two additional macro environmental factors
Institutional and *Ecological*, but they are omitted, to narrow the analysis to the
relevant environment (cp. Narayanan and Fahey 2000, p. 193).

A.3 Segmentation analysis introduction

Porter introduced segmentation analysis, since industries are not homogeneous. The segments are exposed to different competitive forces, exhibiting structural differences, which require varied strategies for competitive advantage (Porter 1985, chapter 7). The segments are defined by buyers type, products variety, channels or geography (Porter 1985, pp. 233-2364):

- **Buyer type:** The types of end buyers that purchase, or could purchase, the industry products

- **Product variety:** The discrete product varieties produced, or could be produced.

In this thesis *geography* is neglected, as virtual worlds are global. *Channel* segments are not considered, because the business models described in this thesis are about *value proposition* only, neglecting *distribution channels*.

A segment is created, if buyer or product differences affect one or more of the five competitive forces. Grant describes the segmentation analysis approach with five steps (Grant 2005, pp. 117-123):

1. **Identify key segmentation variables:** The variables based on buyer type and product variety are identified in subsection 3.2.1. The discussion of inappropriate candidate variables was omitted.

2. **Construct a segmentation matrix:** The 3D segmentation matrix for the virtual 3D world industry can be found on page 48.

3. **Analyze segment attractiveness:** The segment attractiveness is analyzed with *Porter's 5-Forces* described in the next section. This was done for the c-business (4.1.3), i-business (4.2.3) and v-business (4.3.3) case studies.

4. **Identify the segment's key success factors:** The segment specific key success factors were identified in subsection 3.2.2 and evaluated in the course of the case study evaluations in chapter 4.

5. **Select segment scope:** The scope can either be narrow, focusing on one segment or broad, covering multiple segments. The selected segment scope strategies implemented in the case studies were evaluated in chapter 4.

A.4 Porter's 5-Forces structural industry analysis introduction

Porter introduced a structural analysis technique for industries, known as *Porter's 5-Forces*, to assess industry attractiveness (Porter 1998, chapter 1). Each industry or segment attractiveness is determined by the five competitive forces shown in table A.2.

In this thesis *Porter's 5-Forces* are used for analyzing virtual 3D world segment at-

Force threat	Examples for structural determinants
Threat of new entrants	Economies of scale, brand differentiation, capital requirements, distribution networks, cost disadvantages or technological prerequisites.
Rivalry among existing firms	Number of equal competitors, rate of industry growth, high strategic stakes, high exit barriers or information complexity and asymmetry.
Threat of substitute products or services	Relative price performance of substitutes, short technological innovation cycles or perceived level of product differentiation.
Bargaining power of buyers	Undifferentiated products, buyer concentration, switching cost, price sensitivity or threat of backward integration.
Bargaining power of suppliers	Supplier concentration or monopolies, switching cost, supplier's product is key input or threat of forward integration.

Table A.2: Porter's 5-Forces industry analysis

tractiveness to determine threats and opportunities for existing companies. Segment attractiveness analysis differs from industry analysis in terms of *substitutes* and *new entries*:

- **Threat of substitute products or services:** When analyzing substitute products special attention should be paid to substitutes from other segments in comparison to substitutes from other industries.

- **Threat of new entrants:** New entrants do not only include companies outside the industry, but also from other segments. Whereas outside companies have to face *barriers to entry* companies from other segments deal with *barriers to mobility*.

A.5 Value-chain strategy patterns introduction

Heuskel defined the following four distinct value-chain strategy patterns, which can be observed when companies do business by deconstructing and reconstructing the value-chain (Heuskel 1999).

Layer players focus on one value-chain activity, utilize scaling effects and know-

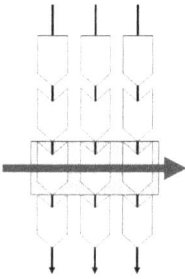

Figure A.1: Layer player pattern

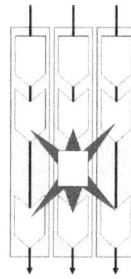

Figure A.2: Market maker pattern

how and usually expand across industry borders (Heuskel 1999, pp. 57-61), while *market makers* introduce new value-chain activities into the existing value-chain and leverage information advantages first throughout the industry and later across industry boundaries (Heuskel 1999, pp. 62-64).

Orchestrators on the other side focus on the core segments, while coordinating

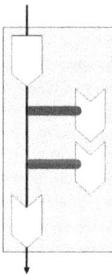

Figure A.3: Orchestrator pattern

Figure A.4: Integrator pattern

the other value-chain activities (Heuskel 1999, pp. 64-68). In contrast to this, *integrators* perform nearly all activities on a value-chain, are seldom supplied by third parties and virtually control the complete value-chain (Heuskel 1999, pp. 68-71).

Appendix B

Expert Interviews with consumers

B.1 Interview approach and qualitative analysis

Interview approach

For this thesis semi-structured and unstructured interviews were used. The following structure was used:

- **General information:** The general questions included questions intended to discover the intensity with which the interview partners participated in virtual worlds in terms of hours per week and years involved.

- **Questions about virtual worlds:** The questions about virtual worlds examined what the interview partners liked or disliked about virtual worlds. Assumed key success factors where also included to be qualitatively verified or falsified. Other questions addressed the interdependencies between virtual worlds, the time consumption and possible integration with real world services.

- **Questions about Second Life:** Those questions were only asked to SL residents. They were targeted to discover the immersion factor of SL, the personal value SL gives to the interview partner and the personal involvement in SL.

- **Questions about success factors of virtual worlds (or Second Life):** Those questions were straight forward and asked about external or general key success factors as well as internal or in-world key success factors. For SL residents this part also included open questions regarding the success of SL as well as future development and company challenges.

The 10 interview partners were chosen from the three customer focus group segments: three interviewees from the *entertainment* segment, one interviewee from the *community* segment and, because of the focus of this thesis, six interviewees from the *business* segment in the form of SL. The interviewees were selected per hand; hence the results cannot be used in a statistical way. Eight interviewees are from Germany, one from United Kingdom and one from the USA.

Eight interviews were conducted through a questionnaire. One was conducted in-world and one via instant messaging system.

Qualitative analysis

The interviews were analyzed in search for qualitative indicators of key success factors. Candidate success factors were separated into in-world and general success factors as can be seen in table B.1. The numbers beside the factors indicate the referencing per virtual world segment. As the interview consists of open questions, the author interpreted some candidate factors within the context.

The general key success factors candidates were clustered into six prerequisites

General key success factors				In-world key success factors			
Candidate	En.	Co.	Bu.	In-world candidate	En.	Co.	Bu.
Network	2	1	2	Immersion	3		3
Graphic	3	1	5	World-wide contacts	1	1	1
Graphic engine	3	1	5	Virtual community	3	1	3
Personalization	1		1	Gameplay	2		
Scalability	2	1	1	User interface	2	1	2
Reliability	2		2	Avatar development	2		1
Response time	1	1	2	World endlessness	2	1	2
Security			1	New content	3		2
Capacity		1	1	Consistent setting	2	1	
Open standards			2	In-world growth	1		1
				Game balance	2		1
				Storyline	2		3
				Freedom of choice	2	1	2
				Building		1	1
				Privacy & security			3

Table B.1: Identification of key success factor candidates

for success, from which the three additional general key success factors referred to on page 32, were derived.

Because the candidate impact differed based on the virtual world segment, the in-world candidates were further analyzed. The clustering into the five key success factors used in the thesis is shown in table B.2.

The evaluation of the candidates, if for example *Gameplay* is essential (X) or just

In-world key success factors

In-world candidate	En.	Co.	Bu.
Immersion factor	H	m	M
World endlessness	X	X	X
Consistent setting	X	X	
In-world growth	X		X
Storyline	X		x
Creativity & freedom	M	m	H
Avatar development	X		X
New content	X		X
Freedom of choice	X	X	X
Building		X	X
Flow experience	H	m	m
Gameplay	X		
User interface	X	X	X
Game balance	X	x	x
Virtual community	H	H	H
World-wide contacts	X	X	X
Virtual community	X	X	X
participant number	X	X	X
Privacy & security	L	m	H

Table B.2: Clustering and determining the impact of in-world success factors

important (x) was determined through analysis of the data from table B.1, additional secondary data sources and the expert knowledge of the author.

By clustering the analysis results into the five in-world key success factors, their impact on the according virtual world segment could be determined to be either high (H), increased (M), medium (m) or low (L). The resulting evaluation is used in figure 3.5 on page 50 as basis for further discussions.

The remainder of appendix B contains the ten interviews conducted.

B.2   Interview with Arc, MMORPG consumer

Arc plays computer games for over 20 years and is actively playing MMORPG for seven years, making him an expert consumer in this subject. The following interview was conducted through a questionnaire:

GENERAL INFORMATION

Name or pseudonym: Arc
Age: 35
Gender: male
How many years do you play MMORPGs?   7
How many hours do you play per week ($\varnothing$ over last 3 months)   15-30h

Questions about virtual worlds

Which virtual worlds do/did you play(ed)?   Everquest, Ultima Online, Anarchy Online, Earth and Beyond, Eve, Horizons, Final Fantasy Online, Dark Age of Camelot, Star Wars Galaxy Online, Lineage II, City of Heroes/Villains, Vanguard, Everquest 2, Lord of the Rings Online, World of Warcraft, Guild Wars, Autoassault, Dungeon Runner.

What do you like about virtual worlds most?   I like the immersion, to be someone you can't be in real live, and the social interaction, meeting people from all over the world to play together. Being able to develop an avatar over a long period of time, and (ideally) never *finish* the game. The extensive gameplay that is offered, questing, fighting, exploring, crafting and socializing.

What do you like about virtual worlds at least?   Stupid players. This kind of games, for me at least, lives by their communities. From socializing, to exploring together, doing missions and quests, fighting the *evil dragon* as it were, all these things depend on the community to be enjoyable for me. *Stupid players* can ruin this fun quite easily for everyone.

Disruptive, malicious, griefing[1] players would probably be a more accurate de-

---
[1]A *griefer* is a slang term used to describe a player in a multi-player video game who plays the game simply to cause grief to other players through harassment (taken from Wikipedia).

scription. This behavior can come in many forms, from disrupting chat channels, *ninja looting*[2], griefing other players, stealing guild property, kill stealing[3], item greed or envy, *training*[4], content blocking, general rudeness, spawn/corpse camping[5], the list goes on (all of which I have seen in my years of playing by the way). Any of these actions diminish my fun and as such are things "I don't like about MMO's". Those are the *stupid players* I referred to.

Do you currently participate in more than one virtual world? No, only *City of Heroes/Villains*.

If no, please give a reason? In my opinion, no matter how much free time you have you can only play one game of this type seriously. They are designed to be time sinks, and reward the player with time spent on them. As such, if you want to accomplish as much as possible in the game, you will spent all your free time on a single game.

If no, can you think of features of virtual worlds or other circumstances which would allow you to participate in more virtual worlds? Not really, these games are designed to *hook* the player, to reward time spent. If done correctly, you don't *want* to spent time on more then one game. You will *want* to keep playing the same game, as time invested is rewarded, and the more time invested the more rewards you will get.

Also, these games benefit strongly from the community; it's more then just logging in and playing a bit (for me). You do meet new people, form friendships; this consumes a fair bit of time, and dividing your attention across several com-

---

[2]A loot ninja or ninja looter, or simply ninja, is a player who takes loot (virtual items like swords, armor, gold, etc.) to which he or she is not entitled (taken from http://www.wowwiki.com/Ninja_Loot).

[3]Kill stealing is rushing to kill a mob some other player was heading toward, just to prevent them from getting credit for killing that creature or to get an item drop before they do. This is especially bad when the mob is somewhat unique or difficult to get to (taken from http://www.wowwiki.com/Kill_Steal).

[4]To *train* another player means in this context to draw a group of monsters into the proximity of another player, so that those monsters attack the unsuspecting player and kill him. It is like being *run over by a train*.

[5]After killing another player, corpse camping is where that player then continues to camp at the enemy's corpse (either by using stealth or other means) and kills them when the player resurrects themselves http://www.wowwiki.com/Corpse_camping).

munities does not work really.

How important is the in-world virtual community for you?   For me, the game stands or falls with them. If the game is great, but you're always alone, you won't last long there. Sure, playing solo is fun, but then it's more of a single player game in the end. While fun, nothing to keep you interested for too long. Even mediocre games, with a great community will keep me playing much longer.

Do you also enter the virtual world just to meet people, or only for questing?   Always a combination: questing *with* friends is much more fun then doing it alone. On the other side of course, just a community, with nothing to do (quests, fighting, whatever) is similar pointless (probably even more so).

How important is changing/new content for you?   Somewhat important. You can only do the same quests, zones, mobs[6] so many times before being bored to tears. New content is needed at a steady rate, to keep me interested.

What do you think of avatar enhancing services between real and virtual world (i.e. buying virtual items)?   I really don't like it for myself. I like to earn my own living within the rules of the game, and be somewhat proud of what I have achieved, be it gold, items or status. I don't care much though if others do it, as long as it doesn't affect my own gameplay (since I don't PvP[7], it doesn't, usually).

What do you think of real services offered in virtual worlds (spanning from marketing of products to services like Pizza ordering)?   Depends on the game world. In a game world that is similar to real live, it fits I think; a Coca-Cola ad in a fantasy setting...no thanks. Immersion is a big factor for me. As such, advertisements, if any, need to fit.

---

[6]Literally *mobile object* is another term for NPC.
[7]The term *Player versus Player* refers to a certain type of game, where players fight each other instead of fighting the computer environment (PvE) in form of monsters or NPC's.

Questions about success factors of virtual worlds

Which are the external success factors in your opinion (please rank them if possible)? Example: network, graphics, package, etc. Network: You need a stable foundation. That includes network, databases etc. These just need to work. No point to a game if you can't even log on, stay connected, or play without too much lag. Also a reliable patch process, to update the clients as needed.

Graphics: To me, very important. The game needs to have a distinct look and feel to it. This doesn't necessarily mean high end graphics, but rather a pleasing, well designed and fitting look to everything.

Character animation and options to appear how you like are similar important. I don't want look as everyone else.

Also, the graphic engine (as well as the network code) needs to be able to handle more then a few players at the same time. No point in looking good in screenshots, when your machine grinds to a halt if more then 10 people are on the screen. These are *massive multiplayer* games after all, so they need to be able to handle it.

Which are the internal success factors in your opinion (please rank them if possible)? Example: Certain in-world setting, rules, characters, professions, etc. The setting is a matter of opinion of course, but no matter what it is, from high fantasy to science faction, it needs to be consistent.

Character development is another vital part of any game of this type. It needs to be fun, fairly balanced, and offer professions/archetypes etc. for different play styles, be it more solo or group orientated. Also, the more options the system offers to build your character individually, the better. This goes both for game mechanics (skills, spells, powers etc) as well as visual looks.

B.3   Interview with Bulvaye, MMORPG consumer

Bulvaye also known as *Winterfee* in *City of Heroes/Villains* is playing MMORPG actively for around six years, making him an expert consumer in this subject. The following interview was conducted through a questionnaire:

GENERAL INFORMATION

Name or pseudonym: Bulvaye aka *Winterfee*
Age: 38.96
Gender: male
How many years do you play MMORPGs?
5-6
How many hours do you play per week (∅ over last 3 months)   10-20h

Questions about virtual worlds

Which virtual worlds do/did you play(ed)?   Dark Age of Camelot, Horizons, Everquest 2, City of Heroes/Villains, World of Warcraft

What do you like about virtual worlds most?   I like to dive into a world that offers heroic possibilities for an avatar who can't get enough of adventures. It's interesting to be part of a persistent world, which continues to evolve with all the avatars, played by other gamers. It's interesting to experience, how in-world economies grows. Also you learn much about the human being and psyche – but this is not always a positive aspect.

What do you like about virtual worlds at least?   To be dependent of other players. It's nice to play your character in groups of other players to discover special areas of the virtual world and experiencing adventures, you were not able to master on your own or just to have fun. But if it wouldn't be possible to play on your own, because you like to do so, or you can't find any suitable group, game play can become frustrating (for me).

Do you currently participate in more than one virtual world?   No, not really.

If no, please give a reason?   The biggest problem is the time you have left (be-sides your *real life*) to spend in MMORPGs. Time is too little and usually online role-playing content plenty. Additionally you have to spend much time to get your character high in level – a motivation throughout the whole game. The higher your level is, the more your character develops his game skills and the more you can explore in the game. It's like the vicious circle: *Just one more level...* (smiles)

If no, can you think of features of virtual worlds or other circumstances which would allow you to participate in more virtual worlds?   I can't imagine fea-tures, which would let me play two MMORPGs at the same time. The most criti-cal factor is time.

How important is the in-world virtual community for you?   It is very impor-tant, because you usually play with other gamers. If you virtually live among a community you can't get along with, you will not team with other players and you will miss an important game aspect.

Do you also enter the virtual world just to meet people, or only for questing? To meet other people virtually, I use other platforms like *forums* or *chats*. It hap-pens that I log into a game and only talk with other players, but my intention is usually to play a game, have fun with the content the game offers and with other players who participate in this interest.

How important is changing/new content for you?   It's very important. If game content is exhausted, you've a kind of *game over* in most online RPGs.

What do you think of avatar enhancing services between real and virtual world (i.e. buying virtual currency or items)?   It's not my way. I don't like to appear with things, I did not earn on my own inside the game – things like items, money or fame.

What do you think of real services offered in virtual worlds (spanning from marketing of products to services like Pizza ordering)?   I would not like commercials in MMORPGs in any kind. If I dive into a virtual world, I don't like to be confronted with real life properties. Instead I wish to feel and think like my avatar would do in this virtual world. He may not know about pizza.

Questions about success factors of virtual worlds

Which are the external success factors in your opinion (please rank them if possible)? (Example: network, graphics, package, etc.) Graphics, graphic engine speed (powered by a fast computer) and quick server response times are responsible for game success. The game engine, storyline and avatar development abilities can be great – but if you have problems to get the feeling, to become immersed into the virtual world, the atmosphere of the world will not surround you and your personal game fun will be very low.

Which are the internal success factors in your opinion (please rank them if possible)? (Example: Certain in-world setting, rules, characters, professions, etc.)

- *Rules and the game balance* are very important. The game system must not be complex, but interesting. There should be many possibilities you develop your avatar without having the feeling, that there is only one best way in the game. Variety in playing styles is important.

- *Storyline:* An interesting story is important for me. I need a story background: Why does my avatar lives in this world? Why does he kill other special mobs? Why are the mobs there and where do they come from? Why should my avatar do certain quests?

- *Gameplay:* Moving through the world, fighting against other mobs and communicating with other players should be easy to handle, intuitive and without delay in game response.

B.4 Interview with Loxagon, MMORPG consumer

Loxagon also known as *Loxà* in *World of Warcraft* is actively playing MMORPG for four years, making him an expert consumer in this subject. The following interview was conducted through a questionnaire:

GENERAL INFORMATION

Name or pseudonym: Loxagon or Loxà
Age: 40
Gender: male
How many years do you play MMORPGs? 4
How many hours do you play per week ($\varnothing$ over last 3 months) 10-35h

Questions about virtual worlds

Which virtual worlds do/did you play(ed)? Dark Age of Camelot, Everquest 2, City of Heroes, World of Warcraft, Guild Wars

What do you like about virtual worlds most? I like adventuring in a fantasy area. I like the possibility to explore, to communicate, to fight and to win or loose, the challenge to survive in an area *unknown*, to check out the character classes and their abilities.

What do you like about virtual worlds at least? A friend of mine once said: *Stupid players!* I can only agree to this.

Do you currently participate in more than one virtual world? No, only World of Warcraft.

If no, please give a reason? No other game is as attractive as WoW for me.

If no, can you think of features of virtual worlds or other circumstances which would allow you to participate in more virtual worlds? Yes; two or more interconnected worlds, with character transfer and the possibility of transparent character enhancement. Wouldn't it be nice to travel from WoW to Everquest 2 or another world!?

How important is the in-world virtual community for you? I can't imagine playing a game in which the community doesn't fit. It makes no sense to struggle every minute over people you don't want to struggle over in the first place.

Do you also enter the virtual world just to meet people, or only for questing? Sometimes, but most to play.

How important is changing/new content for you? It's important. For a while you can play the same content with other classes, but after a wile it becomes boring without new content.

What do you think of avatar enhancing services between real and virtual world (i.e. buying virtual currency or items)? It's one way to save time, but it is not my way. Like I said "It's a game!" and I have no fun if the game is over quicker and I paid for it on top.

What do you think of real services offered in virtual worlds (spanning from marketing of products to services like Pizza ordering)? Nothing.

Questions about success factors of virtual worlds

Which are the external success factors in your opinion (please rank them if possible)? (Example: network, graphics, package, etc.) Graphics are most important. The combination of landscape, virtual items and NPCs or avatars must harmonize. The graphic style must be consistent. In that, it is not relevant if the graphics are not realistic, if the exaggerations sum up to a distinguishable individuality. This is mandatory especially for the avatar. In some virtual worlds, the possibilities offered to modeling the avatar face are excessive and basically unimportant, because they do not attract attention during interaction.

Which are the internal success factors in your opinion (please rank them if possible)? (Example: Certain in-world setting, rules, characters, professions, etc.)
For me *gameplay* is paramount. The user interface must be intuitive and easy to remember, without taking all challenge from the user. In this regard, Blizzard has always set new quality standards with all their products so far. Sometimes, I ask myself, why other companies with similar games did it differently. In my opinion, this key success factor primarily decides, if a virtual world reaches *Kultstatus*.

Figure B.1: The *Scorpions* follow Loxà to new adventures and mayhem

B.5   Interview with Ariadne, virtual world owner in AW

Ariadne is the world owner of *Crete*, one of the numerous AW worlds. The following interview was conducted in-world at the beach in front of the queen's palace of ancient Crete:

GENERAL INFORMATION

Name or pseudonym: Ariadne
Age: 28
Gender: female
How many years do you participate in virtual worlds?   3
How many hours do you spend per week (∅ over last 3 months)   50-70h

Questions about virtual worlds

Which virtual worlds do/did you play(ed)?   ActiveWorlds

What do you like about virtual worlds most?   I like to be able to express myself creatively without restrictions. I like to design landscapes and building and I have a great interest in the ancient Minoan culture, so that I made this RPG[8] virtual world within AW.

What do you like about virtual worlds at least?   I dislike technical restrictions to my creativity. You are limited in some ways as to what you can create here due to network lag so you have to limit the objects and the detail on them in order to not cause other visitors PCs to crash or to slow down.

Do you consider this building ability as the main advantage over normal chatrooms and MMORPG, where you can play but not create?   Oh yes absolutely!

---

[8]Role-Playing Game

In Second Life, you can also build, but for persistent structures you have to pay more than just a monthly subscription fee like in AW. How much do you pay for an own world? That depends on the size of the world and I think there are some things about it that should be changed. You have to pay for citizens to come into you world as well as the world itself. I think that you should be able to have as many AW citizens able to come into the world as they want. At the moment I pay for 10 simultaneous users. If more users than that wish to enter my world and it is at full capacity they can not.

Do you currently participate in more than one virtual world? No

If no, please give a reason? Well due to the fact that I am building a world by myself and with the real life things I do, time is scarce. But I really do like AW a lot. On occasion I do go to other virtual worlds sometimes to "play" and relax, though very rare (laughs). If they were connected I would possibly participate in more worlds.

How important is the in-world virtual community for you? Very important!

Do you consider it to be a critical success factor for the world itself? Well of course, unless I was building a world for myself, which many do. I myself have created an RPG which isn't just your normal chat world; it is for many people to come and play and to enjoy. Alas RPG bots[9] are not inexpensive and to implement the ideas I have come up with has been a very long process.

So your main focus is on building and world creating, but you also enjoy it, when others have fun within your creation? Yes also the ideas of the RPG itself, not just the building of the world but all of it is much more tedious with a RPG than it is in a regular chat world.

In MMORPG worlds they constantly make content updates, to keep users interested. Do you think, this is important also for AW? Sure... people get bored

---

[9]Short for *robots*, synonymous to NPC

easily, so I think you have to make it fun. This is also the reason I have opened my world before the RPG is completely finished so that people can experience the growth of the world.

What do you think of real services offered in virtual worlds (spanning from marketing of products to services like Pizza ordering)? I think it is a wonderful idea. There are many things you can do in virtual worlds: have meetings with people in real time from all over the world and enjoy an *atmosphere* while doing it.

Do you think, this is superior compared to offering these services through a normal website? If yes why? For example take this interview here. We are on the beach with a beautiful sky... it makes it more *real* than a regular website, don't you agree? There are many ideas I have for this type of thing that will be implemented in the future: You can open a scroll or book and order things then move on to the next object and order from that. Many things can be done, as I have said, we are only limited by our imagination.

Yes, I do agree, that it is more real of course. But I also heard arguments, that i.e. this *hampers* the immersive experience. What do you answer to them? Perhaps they should have a more open mind! An office building is like a cage but if you could have your meeting on a beach you would not feel as if you were *caged* as much, in my arrogant opinion.

What you say about office cages reminds me of the movie *Office Space*, where the main character asked a hypnotist, if he can hypnotize him, so he would think, he was out fishing all day. (laughs) So he could if he were here!!!

What about the argument, that 3D does not enhance the information flow of say Wikipedia articles? Well... let me ask you this: If you read an article on ancient Crete versus coming to this world and experiencing things that they had which would you learn more from? To see the olive masher at work versus being told in words how it worked with limited 2D pictures?

This is a difficult question. As I read many books, I have come to this problematic: If you read a novel you imagine certain pictures is your mind. If this book becomes a film you either like it, or dislike it, as it did not match your imagination.   Yes but that is fiction and it is wonderful to imagine. If you were researching, to experience it as if you were there tends to make things sink in more.

I see your point: reading an article about some mechanic or archaeological subject, I mostly like the computer generated visualization, as it is more immersive, than looking at some withered rock and reading 30 pages.   Yes! (laughs) Most MMORPG's are based on fiction too, but there are many things that can be done.

Questions about success factors of virtual worlds

Coming back to virtual worlds: Which are the external success factors in your opinion (please rank them if possible)? Example: network, graphics, package, etc.   Well you might want to ask someone else on that, who is more experienced in many other platforms...I have only used AW. Perhaps you could answer that question better than I since you have been to many other platforms.

I ask this question also to other experts. For me your personal opinion is important on this.   Well, I think both, network and graphics are important. Actually if anything limits or hampers the creativity of a world then it should be addressed! For example let's take a chair object: In the action field of the model you can put codes that create effects, so you can make it a pass through or solid, so persons can not pass through the object. Sadly more codes in action fields create more graphic and network lag too. So when you have an RPG you have to be very careful not to have to many objects with codes, because the bot uses codes in everything that a person can interact with.

Which would bring us back to another external success factor: the game or world engine?   Yes, the less power the engine has, the more restrictions on the imagination.

Which are the internal success factors in your opinion (please rank them if possible)? Example: Certain in-world setting, rules, characters, possibilities, etc. Do you mean for my world or all the worlds in AW in general because they all differ?

For your world, as well as AW. Hmmm, I'm not sure I can answer that one either... (laughs) Maybe we could come back to that question?

As far as I understood you, one internal success factor would be the ability to build own stuff. Yes and to experience real time chat with people such as yourself on the other side of the world while being in an environment. The environment of the world is its success and also the people in it. But you see for some of these worlds, people do not make them for others to enjoy. They do it for themselves. So the success is in the eye of the beholder I suppose and how far and how much work a world owner is willing to put in.

So the environment as content is an important success factor? Yes it is. Many do not know how to make models for their worlds so they are limited to *buying* the objects.

So if they lack the skills to do it themselves, they have to pay for it. Just like in the real world, where people can either buy a house or construct it by themselves. True ... limited by that for sure. But there are extremes here: You have *Gor* worlds; worlds were they pay you to kill people.

They pay me to kill others? Yes! (laughs) You must go around killing people and get as much money as you can. The person with the most money at the end of the week becomes king or queen.

I assume, I get more money, the more gore and splatter there is? Well you steal the money by killing. I didn't like that much. I was a lead builder there and its fun to have a *war* mode once in a while with prior notice, but many people do not like losing what they worked for. (laughs)

What money? Where did the killed people acquired the money?   Fishing, mining, etc. Same as here in Crete. You will be able to kill and gain the person's money soon, if they didn't put it in the bank. But I will make it so, that you are safe unless you are in combat mode. If you click on me right now you can't kill me. You will only see my description. But also here you can work a job to make money, fish and mine and buy and sell things.

A world, where you enjoy it, if some thief steals your money. It's like in the old movies in New York, except that the killed ones never seemed very happy about it...   Yes (laughs), but here you can come back to revamp your losses.

This would be even less funny in worlds like Entropia Universe or Second Life, where you can actually count the losses in real US-$.   But in my world if you make choices that were not morally cool, you will come back as something not human and you can not do a thing except eat which sort of stops those who would do things that would harm other citizens.

That was my last question. Thank you for your precious time!   You have a great day!!!

Figure B.2: Ariadne and Edagener after the interview at the harbor entrance

B.6   Interview with Thorsten Seelowe, SL resident

Thorsten Seelowe participates on behalf of his employer in SL. Though he is not that active within the world, he has a deep understanding of IT architectures and their business value. The following interview was conducted through Sametime, an instant messaging application from IBM:

GENERAL INFORMATION

Name or pseudonym: Thorsten Seelowe
Age: 35
Gender: male
How many years do you play MMORPGs?
Less than one year
How many hours do you play per week ($\varnothing$ over last 3 months)   1h

Questions about virtual worlds

Which virtual worlds did/do you play(ed)?   Second Life and Metaverse.

Do you visit virtual worlds for private or business reasons?   Business reasons only.

What do you like about virtual worlds most?   Flying (laughs) Interactive objects (like cars, hotels, kitchens), being able to view them from all perspectives.

What do you like least about virtual worlds?   From a social perspective: Virtual crime and rip-off. It's not worse than the bad sides of the 2D Internet, but it's also not an improvement. From a technical perspective: A new mandatory client download almost every week. Bad server performance/capacities.

What do you mean by bad server capacity?   The maximum number of avatars per SL island (e.g. 40). The platform currently can't really host big conventions.

But SL marketing says that the virtual world of Second Life does not have restrictions of maximum users, as MMORPG worlds like World of Warcraft

do. What do you think of this?   It's only half the story: The SL *world* as a whole
scales, if Linden Lab adds physical hardware to host an island. But the scaling
is limited per island. See e.g. the article from Frank Rose on this subject (Rose
2007), or try to visit a famous island at prime time... (frowns)

**Immersion is one of the most important characteristics of virtual worlds in
general. Do you experience immersion in Second Life?**   The visuals and audio
is really fine, but personally I don't feel immersed as long as it's *just my standard
computer* in front of me. It's okay, but more immersion would require special
VR-devices.

Did you ever felt immersed by video games?   I felt partly immersed by a 3D adventure game with a really good plot. (I don't remember the name of the game).
I never played ego shooters that might provide deeper immersion.

**What is in your opinion the difference between a 3D adventure game and Sec-
ond Life, that lets you immerse into the one but not into the other (reasons can
be in-world or outside)?**   The 3D adventure game had a really good story. The
player had to solve mystique riddles. These were created by professional story
writers. The visuals were basic. I played that game on my Amiga from Com-
modore those days. SL on the other hand has superior visuals, but the story is
often boring, e.g. empty buildings, theme parks without visitors. A lot of avatars
just sit around and do small talk. I can have the same chat with my favorite instant messaging solution (e.g. Sametime 7.5) and don't need a high-end graphics
card.

Did you ever spend some money on your avatar or something else?   You mean
real $ or € for L$ to buy something in SL? No, but I think it okay to do so. If people
spend US-$ to play with a real life slot machine or video game, why shouldn't
they pay for goodies in SL?

Questions about success factors of virtual worlds

Okay, lets go now to the last part of the interview, which is about success factors for virtual worlds: You stated, that you spend only one hour per week in Second Life. Why is that so? Because the current business values is somewhat limited. However the 2D Internet started the same. I believe virtual worlds will become more valuable in the future.

For what reasons? I like the idea to visit my next potential holiday resort upfront in SL. Today I use *Google Earth* to check the size of the beach, but I can't look inside the hotel. Another use case would be to *test drive* my next kitchen or the look and feel of a new living room. Those offering are currently prototyped in SL and I hope they will be successful.

Which are the external success factors in your opinion (please rank them if possible)? Example: network, graphics, package, etc.

1. Stability and capacity of the platform.

2. Open standard for 3D worlds. I don't like monopolies.

3. Stable clients available on all platforms. Not just Windows, but also for Linux and MacOS – with a wide range of graphic adapters.

Which are the internal success factors in your opinion (please rank them if possible)? Example: Certain in-world setting, rules, characters, professions, etc.

1. Privacy and Security, e.g. secure group meetings.

2. Value-add offerings, not just advertisement channels.

Do you think Second Life will be the place to be for the future, or will only the concept survive? The concept will survive and SL will be one of the places in the future realizing that concept. Altavista was the de facto Internet search engine and along came Google.

What prerequisite is needed to make virtual 3D worlds the next step, which will replaces 2D Internet, like 2D Internet replaced the command line interface Internet nearly 20 years ago? Or will it not replace 2D Internet? It won't! (laughing) I still love my ssh login[10] from all over the world. No 3D *game* can replace the crispness of the command line.

So virtual 3D worlds will stay just *games*? No, similar to the 2D Internet, which is much more that just an information library today. But 3D needs to add value. If I want to execute a money transaction, I don't want to use my avatar to walk to a virtual ATM and touch-type the account information. But I can't get immersed by my next holiday resort using ASCII graphics[11].

So the challenge for businesses investing in virtual 3D worlds will be to think about how they can leverage the third dimension? Yes!

Thorsten, thank you for your time and your concise answers. You're welcome. See you in SL! (smiles)

---

[10]The *ssh login* is a text based interface to log into Unix/Linux computers. The Windows analogy of this interface is the MS-DOS *Command Prompt*, though not so comprehensive like *ssh login*.

[11]*ASCII graphics* are graphics, which are done using normal characters, for example ":-)" for a smiley.

B.7   Interview with Reliciente Starbrook, SL resident

Reliciente Starbrook participates on behalf of her employer in SL. Though she also is not that active within the world, she has a deep understanding of IT architectures and the business perspective. The following interview was conducted through a questionnaire:

GENERAL INFORMATION

Name or pseudonym: Reliciente Starbrook
Age: 43
Gender: female
How many years do you play MMORPGs?
Less than one year
How many hours do you play per week ($\varnothing$ over last 3 months)   3-4h

Questions about virtual worlds

Which virtual worlds did/do you play(ed)?   Second Life only.

Do you visit virtual worlds for private or business reasons?   Business reasons only.

What do you like about virtual worlds most?   I like being able to do things which are physically impossible in real worlds.

What don't you like about virtual worlds?   The lack of privacy due to the presence awareness.

Do you currently participate in more than one virtual world?   No, because of lack of time and I already sit in front of a screen for more than 12 hours a day – I could not imagine increasing this time.

If no, can you think of features of virtual worlds or other circumstances which would allow you to participate in more virtual worlds?   Lighter-weight client in contrast to the current Second Life client – as it is not possible to multi-task in Second Life while running processor or memory intensive applications – this includes VoIP clients.

How important is the in-world virtual community for you?   I feel a strong connection only to the people in the virtual community which I have met already in real life – as I do not like interacting with strangers, because I do not know their motives or as is often the case – their language.

Do you also enter the virtual world just to meet people, or only for questing? I enter for questing and experimenting (i.e. scripting).

How important is changing/new content for you?   I actually think that some areas should not change content. My life is full of change – therefore some areas should offer some familiarity for the user.

What do you think of avatar enhancing services between real and virtual world (i.e. buying virtual currency or items)?   I think it is a great business opportunity for those people selling, but I personally have a hard time spending much money on virtual items.

What do you think of real services offered in virtual worlds (spanning from marketing of products to services like Pizza ordering)?   I would not order pizza in Second Life, as it is much easier from a usability stand point to order it on the Internet or simply over the telephone. There are some things which make more sense to sell in a true 3D environment – such as homes, hotels and clothing.

Questions about Second Life

Immersion is one of the most important characteristics of virtual worlds in general. Do you experience immersion in Second Life?   No, I am always aware that I am using a laptop – this is partly due to the performance of the Second Life client.

If no, did you ever felt immersion into video games? If yes why? If no, why?
Yes, felt immersion with video games, as they are fast moving with matching performance. You also have a goal to reach (stealing an egg or reaching the end of the world) so that you are concentrating on reaching that goal and thereby become immersed.

If yes, what is in your opinion the difference between a (3D adventure) game and Second Life, that lets you immerse into the one but not into the other?
Performance is better with a 3D game and the graphics are better. Second Life has few rules and no objectives, whereas you typically have a goal or objectives to meet with other games.

Did you ever spend some money on your avatar or something else in world?
Yes, but it was very minimal and the money had been given to me by another avatar.

What is in your opinion the value Second Life gives you?   For me personally it forces me to think of new ways to design user interfaces and to experiment with a new user interface.

Questions about success factors of Second Life

Which are the external success factors in your opinion (please rank them if possible)? (Examples: network, graphics, package, etc.)

1. More reliability – many objects disappear in Second Life – regardless of whether you bought them or painstakingly acquired or made them – that will cause people to give up on Second Life.

2. Lighter-weight client – downloading occurs often and it is a large client.

3. Performance – when driving a car – you can overtake the scenery and are suddenly in a place, where the environment has disappeared or no one has clothes on.

4. Graphics – to successfully sell real world items in Second Life – they must look more realistic.

Which are the internal success factors in your opinion (please rank them if possible)? (Examples: Certain in-world setting, rules, characters, professions, etc.) Monetary security must be maintained – potentially there will be a need for brokerage firms to buy things so that the buyer can have the right to return things and the user knows that the user is there tomorrow. In particular this would be necessary for buying any real life items, as anyone could create an avatar and then disappear tomorrow.

Do you think Second Life will be the place to be for the future, or will only the concept survive? For Second Life to become a 3D Internet venue it must solve the problems identified above or it will be a nice toy with a nice concept.

What prerequisite is needed to make virtual 3D worlds the next step, which will replaces 2D Internet, like 2D Internet replaced the command line interface Internet nearly 20 years ago? Or will it not replace 2D Internet? Some things do not lend themselves to 3D such as written text – even with the advent of the web page things such as books (or a piece of paper) have been around for thousands of years and are still in use today in spite of alternative technologies. It is simply easier to transport and easy to start (open the book or look at the page). If you have a small device which allows you to rapidly turn it on and access the information you need (mobile) – then you can perhaps think of getting rid of books.

Will virtual 3D worlds stay just *games*? The may grow into mainstream business – depending upon whether they fulfill the requirements I mentioned above.

What is the main challenge for businesses investing in virtual 3D worlds? Determine whether there really is a market for their goods or services in a 3D world.

B.8   Interview with Joe Triskaidekaphobia, SL resident

Joe Triskaidekaphobia participates on behalf of his employer in SL. He is very active in the Second Life where he is involved in object design, scripting and back-end application implementation for client solutions. The following interview was conducted through a questionnaire:

GENERAL INFORMATION

Name or pseudonym: Joe Triskaidekaphobia
Age: n/a
Gender: n/a
How many years do you play MMORPGs?
Less than one year
How many hours do you play per week ($\varnothing$ over last 3 months)   40-45h

Questions about virtual worlds

Which virtual worlds did/do you play(ed)?   Second Life only.

Do you visit virtual worlds for private or business reasons?   Business reasons only. If those reasons are no more, my SL participation will decrease probably to zero hours per week. But maybe if I get to now Second Life better, I probably would end up spending some time in there.

What do you like about virtual worlds most?   Have seen only SL – there it is the extensibility.

What don't you like about virtual worlds?   That they become a mirror of our society.

Do you currently participate in more than one virtual world?   No.

If no, please give a reason?   Because I use SL for business reasons – as soon as business requires me to participate in another one, I'll do it.

How important is the in-world virtual community for you? Not at all.

Do you also enter the virtual world just to meet people, or only for questing?
n/a

How important is changing/new content for you? Not at all.

What do you think of avatar enhancing services between real and virtual world (i.e. buying virtual currency or items)? I cannot understand people doing that (smiles).

What do you think of real services offered in virtual worlds (spanning from marketing of products to services like Pizza ordering)? Well, compared to a *traditional* website, starting the SL client just to order a pizza seem to be a bit overkill.

Questions about Second Life

Immersion is one of the most important characteristics of virtual worlds in general. Do you experience immersion in Second Life? Not at all.

If no did you ever felt immersion into video games? If yes why? If no, why?
n/a

If yes, what is in your opinion the difference between a (3D adventure) game and Second Life, that lets you immerse into the one but not into the other?
n/a

Did you ever spend some money on your avatar or something else in world?
Yep, upload of textures as I needed these to creating a business presence.

What is in your opinion the value Second Life gives you? Not sure about any value to me other than the fact that I love to build applications and suddenly end up doing this in SL.

Questions about success factors of Second Life

Which are the external success factors in your opinion (please rank them if possible)? (Examples: network, graphics, package, etc.) First graphics, second network – may change in rank, but in general the user experience.

Which are the internal success factors in your opinion (please rank them if possible)? (Example: Certain in-world setting, rules, characters, professions, etc.) n/a

Do you think Second Life will be the place to be for the future or will only the concept survive? I tend to believe that Second Life might be for the 3D-world what Mosaic was for the 2D-world: The first half-way working implementation of a concept. Whether it will survive or not and in what form – nobody knows. Mosaic has survived as the code base for modern browsers far longer as people believe.

What prerequisite is needed to make virtual 3D worlds the next step, which will replaces 2D Internet, like 2D Internet replaced the command line interface Internet nearly 20 years ago? Or will it not replace 2D Internet? CPU power, bandwidth, and some value added for the visitors. The step from command line to 2D is bigger, because it enabled more people to make use of the Internet. The step from 2D to 3D is a technological challenge, but has not that impact on the users to do something which they could not do before.

Will virtual 3D worlds stay just *games*? No, they will find an area where it makes sense to interact in 3D.

What is the main challenge for businesses investing in virtual 3D worlds? Change mindset – do not copy what you have done in 2D to 3D – I have seen far too many *PowerPoint* presentations in SL. I still believe that the only real viewer for such a presentation is *PowerPoint*, not the Second Live client. It is boring and undermines the additional value a 3D world can bring.

B.9 Interview with Estate Miles, SL resident

Estate Miles, organized and executed IBM's *Girls' Day 2007* activities in SL (IBM 2007b). In this, girls from high school are introduced to new technologies to become motivated to enter technology professions, when they graduate in the future. The following interview was conducted through a questionnaire:

GENERAL INFORMATION

Name/pseudonym: Estate Miles
Age: 34
Gender: female
How many years do you play MMORPGs?
0.5
How many hours do you play per week ($\varnothing$ over last 3 months) 0h

Questions about virtual worlds

Which virtual worlds did/do you play(ed)? Second Life

Do you visit virtual worlds for private or business reasons? Business reasons only.

What do you like about virtual worlds most? That it is more like the real world. The barrier to talk to unknown people is lower than in regular chat programs.

What don't you like about virtual worlds? That it is additional time I spend in front of the computer, since I sit in front of a computer the whole day at work.

Do you currently participate in more than one virtual world? No.

If no, please give a reason? I rather spend my time in real life.

If no, can you think of features of virtual worlds or other circumstances which would allow you to participate in more virtual worlds? It should rather be like the Internet. There should be just one virtual world that connects all virtual worlds and I can move between the worlds with one avatar.

How important is the in-world virtual community for you? Not too important.

Do you also enter the virtual world just to meet people, or only for questing? Depends; currently just for questing.

How important is changing/new content for you? Very, if it is used for information purposes.

What do you think of avatar enhancing services between real and virtual world (i.e. buying virtual currency or items)? This is very important for doing business, i.e. buying things for the real life.

What do you think of real services offered in virtual worlds (spanning from marketing of products to services like Pizza ordering)? This is a good thing, because Second Life is closer to the real life, than the 2D Internet and new products can be evaluated better than in the Internet.

Questions about Second Life

Immersion is one of the most important characteristics of virtual worlds in general. Do you experience immersion in Second Life? Not really.

If no did you ever felt immersion into video games? If yes why? If no, why? No. I do not know why not.

Did you ever spend some money on your avatar or something else in world? No.

What is in your opinion the value Second Life gives you? To see things in a more realistic way than just on a picture in the Internet. When shopping or interacting with people, it is more realistic in Second Life than in the Internet.

Questions about success factors of Second Life

Which are the external success factors in your opinion (please rank them if possible)? (Examples: network, graphics, package, etc.)   Graphics, as better graphics make the virtual world more realistic.

Which are the internal success factors in your opinion (please rank them if possible)? (Example: Certain in-world setting, rules, characters, professions, etc.)   The number of participants. The more people use Second Life, the more valuable it gets.

Do you think Second Life will be the place to be for the future or will only the concept survive?   I think the concept will survive. It will get more open and will not just be sponsored by one company like Linden Lab.

What prerequisite is needed to make virtual 3D worlds the next step, which will replaces 2D Internet, like 2D Internet replaced the command line interface Internet nearly 20 years ago? Or will it not replace 2D Internet?   Both technologies will exist. It will depend on the type of interaction which of the two technologies will be used.

Will virtual 3D worlds stay just *games*?   It will be like the Internet. People will use it for social interaction, information and shopping.

What is the main challenge for businesses investing in virtual 3D worlds? The number of people using it.

B.10   Interview with SL resident

This SL resident is participates on behalf of his employer in SL. He is very active in the Second Life where he is involved in object design, scripting and back-end application implementation for client solutions. The following interview was conducted through a questionnaire:

GENERAL INFORMATION

Name or pseudonym: n/a
Age: 35
Gender: male
How many years do you play MMORPGs? 5
How many hours do you play per week (∅ over last 3 months) 8h

Questions about virtual worlds

Which virtual worlds did/do you play(ed)?   Guild Wars, WoW, Dark Age of Camelot, Second Life (which is not really a MMORPG)

What do you like about virtual worlds most?   Freedom of choice.

What don't you like about virtual worlds?   Monthly costs.

Do you currently participate in more than one virtual world?   Yes.

How important is the in-world virtual community for you?   Depends on their influence on the game.

Do you also enter the virtual world just to meet people, or only for questing?   Rather for questing.

How important is changing/new content for you?   It is not so important for me.

What do you think of avatar enhancing services between real and virtual world (i.e. buying virtual currency or items)?   It is a good business opportunity.

What do you think of real services offered in virtual worlds (spanning from marketing of products to services like Pizza ordering)?   Depends on the world. In games I dislike it. In virtual worlds like SL it might be beneficial.

Questions about Second Life

Immersion is one of the most important characteristics of virtual worlds in general. Do you experience immersion in Second Life?   *NO!!!*

If no did you ever felt immersion into video games? If yes why? If no, why?   Yes, because you have a world and a story based in and around the world.

If yes, what is in your opinion the difference between a (3D adventure) game and Second Life, that lets you immerse into the one but not into the other?   Well, there are three differences:

1. Missing story

2. Miserable graphics so far

3. SL is all about business and not so much about experience

Did you ever spend some money on your avatar or something else in world?   Yes

What is in your opinion the value Second Life gives you?   At the moment it is more of a hype than real business. But I think this will change over time.

Questions about success factors of Second Life

Which are the external success factors in your opinion (please rank them if possible)? (Examples: network, graphics, package, etc.)   Initial cost, graphics, ease of use and freedom of choice.

Which are the internal success factors in your opinion (please rank them if possible)? (Example: Certain in-world setting, rules, characters, professions, etc.)   The storyline, award systems and professions.

Do you think Second Life will be the place to be for the future or will only the concept survive? The concept will, but SL will certainly have to change dramatically.

What prerequisite is needed to make virtual 3D worlds the next step, which will replaces 2D Internet, like 2D Internet replaced the command line interface Internet nearly 20 years ago? Or will it not replace 2D Internet? I do not think it will replace it. Generally it is faster way to do business, searches, registrations, etc. in 2D. 3D is rather a place for immersive experiences that 2D can't offer.

Will virtual 3D worlds stay just *games*? No.

What is the main challenge for businesses investing in virtual 3D worlds?

1. Overcome prejudices and image problems of 3D worlds.

2. Find lucrative and sound business models.

B.11   Interview with Spook Widdershins, SL resident

Spook Widdershins participates on behalf of his employer in SL. His interest in Second Life is primarily fueled by interest in new technologies. The following interview was conducted through a questionnaire:

GENERAL INFORMATION

Name or pseudonym: Spook Widdershins
Age: 29
Gender: male
How many years do you play MMORPGs? 1
How many hours do you play per week ($\varnothing$ over last 3 months) 2h

Questions about virtual worlds

Which virtual worlds did/do you play(ed)? Second Life

Do you visit virtual worlds for private or business reasons? Business reasons.

What do you like about virtual worlds most? The level of interaction and self-expression you can achieve make things a lot more realistic and personal. They make even relatively mundane things fun.

What don't you like about virtual worlds? In the case of Second Life, I really don't like the fact that you frequently have to download a new client application in order to access the world.

Do you currently participate in more than one virtual world? No.

If no, please give a reason? It takes a fair amount of time and effort even using just one virtual world. I don't have a lot of spare time so one virtual world is more than enough for me.

If no, can you think of features of virtual worlds or other circumstances which would allow you to participate in more virtual worlds? Greater interoperability between the virtual worlds would be a good start, particularly with respect to the client software needed to access a virtual world (i.e. don't want to run a separate client for each world). As a start, using a common user interface so that people can quickly get involved with other virtual worlds would be a good step in the right direction.

How important is the in-world virtual community for you? Most of the reason for my using Second Life is based around work and doing specific projects. Consequently, the in-world community is not particularly important for me.

Do you also enter the virtual world just to meet people, or only for questing? I use it primarily to meet with other colleagues who are in different parts of the (real) world.

How important is changing/new content for you? I think this is extremely important, particularly for demonstrations and education scenarios where creating 3D models etc. can really help people to understand a particular subject.

What do you think of avatar enhancing services between real and virtual world (i.e. buying virtual currency or items)? Personally, I don't see the value in using real money to purchase virtual items. To me it is money lost.

What do you think of real services offered in virtual worlds (spanning from marketing of products to services like Pizza ordering)? I think it's a good thing and an obvious thing for companies to do – if you can order a pizza from a website, why shouldn't you be able to do the same thing from within a virtual world as well. Plus the user has more possibilities for interaction when it comes to procuring products/services in a virtual world.

Questions about Second Life

Immersion is one of the most important characteristics of virtual worlds in general. Do you experience immersion in Second Life? I find the interface a bit tricky at times, particularly to move around the environment – this spoils the effect of immersion I think.

If no did you ever felt immersion into video games? If yes why? If no, why? I've felt more immersed in first-person computer games – it's the combination of smooth/natural movement around the virtual environment plus sound effects to match. While quite old now, *Doom* was a good early example of immersion in a computer game – and it was much down to a story line that you follow as you go through.

If yes, what is in your opinion the difference between a (3D adventure) game and Second Life, that lets you immerse into the one but not into the other? See above – for me, it is following a plot line and striving towards a goal.

Did you ever spend some money on your avatar or something else in world? Yes – mainly clothes and other items to personalize my avatar.

What is in your opinion the value Second Life gives you? It gives me an open environment in which I can create new content and share this with other people.

Questions about success factors of Second Life

Which are the external success factors in your opinion (please rank them if possible)? (Examples: network, graphics, package, etc.)

1. *Graphics* – most people have a decent graphics card these days.

2. *Network* – most people have broadband and can therefore use more network intensive applications.

Which are the internal success factors in your opinion (please rank them if possible)? (Example: Certain in-world setting, rules, characters, professions, etc.)

1. *Communities* – the ability to meet like-minded people and socialize with them.

2. *Ability to personalize* experience of the virtual world, such as by customizing your avatar or creating new content

3. *Lots of space*, so the user feels like they can wander around endlessly without feeling boxed-in.

Do you think Second Life will be the place to be for the future or will only the concept survive?   I think Second Life is a starting point but it is likely to be succeeded by something else.

What prerequisite is needed to make virtual 3D worlds the next step, which will replaces 2D Internet, like 2D Internet replaced the command line interface Internet nearly 20 years ago? Or will it not replace 2D Internet?   The web browser was integrated into the operating system, which led to the rise of the 2D Internet – suddenly everyone could access it. For the same to be true with virtual worlds a similar thing might need to happen and this will require some form of standardization – for example, a common client application used to access the virtual worlds (maybe a *virtual worlds* browser?)

Will virtual 3D worlds stay just *games*?   No, I think they are the next logic step in the evolution of the Internet and will probably replace all the separate applications we use today - web browser, instant messaging client, etc. People will just access the 3D Internet instead. Virtual worlds do have some way to go though before this happens.

What is the main challenge for businesses investing in virtual 3D worlds? The sheer number of virtual worlds out there means that it is impossible to reach all of their target clients, without creating a presence in each separate world. This likely limits some of the investments in 3D worlds.

Bibliography

Aarseth, Espen, "How We Became Postdigital - From CyberStudies to Game Studies," in Silver, David and Massanari, Adrienne, eds., *Critical cyberculture studies*, New York: New York University Press, 2006, chapter 3, pp. 37–46.

Berman, Saul J., Steven Abraham, Bill Battino, Louisa Shipnuck, and Andreas Neus, "Navigationg the media divide – Innovating and enabling new business models," Strategic View G510-6579-03, IBM Institute for Business Value, Somers, NY, USA , February 15th, 2007.

Billhardt, Sonja, "Geliebte Zockerbande," *Focus*, 2007, *vol. 14* (no. 19), pp. 142–145.

Bonnett, Kendra R., *An IBM guide to doing business on the Internet*, New York: McGraw-Hill, 2000.

Brun, Jeremy, Farzad Safaei, and Paul Boustead, "Managing Latency and Fairness in Networked Games," *Communications of the ACM*, November 2006, *vol. 49* (no. 11), pp. 46–51.

Casati, Rebecca, Matthias Matussek, Philipp Oehmke, and Moritz von Uslar, "Alles im Wunderland," *Der Spiegel*, 17. Februar 2007, *vol. 60* (no. 8), pp. 150–163.

Cass, Stephen, "Exploring the third dimension," *IEEE Spectrum*, February 2007, *vol. 44* (no. 2), p. 50.

Castronova, Edward, *Synthetic worlds: The business and culture of online games*, Chicago: The University of Chicago Press, 2005.

Chen, Jenova, "Flow in Games (and Everything Else)," *Communications of the ACM*, April 2007, *vol. 50* (no. 4), pp. 31–34.

Chen, Kuan-Ta, Polly Huang, and Chin-Laung Lei, "How Sensitive are Online Gamers to Network Quality," *Communications of the ACM*, November 2006, *vol. 49* (no. 11), pp. 34–38.

Claypool, Mark and Kajal Claypool, "Latency and Player Actions in Online Games," *Communications of the ACM*, November 2006, *vol. 49* (no. 11), pp. 40–45.

DeMarco, Michael, Eric Lesser, and Tony O'Driscoll, "Leadership in a distributed world – Lessons from online gaming," IBV study G510-6611-00, IBM Institute for Business Value, Somers, NY , June 12th, 2007.

Doppler, Klaus and Christoph Lauterburg, *Change Management: Den Unternehmenswandel gestalten*, 11. ext. and updated ed., Campus Verlag, August 2005.

Fink, Dietmar and Bianka Knoblach, *Die großen Management Consultants – Ihre Geschichte, ihre Kompetenz, ihre Strategien*, Verlag Franz Vahlen, 2003.

Fung, Anthony, "Bridging Cyberlife and Real Life - A Study of Online Communities in Hong Kong," in Silver, David and Massanari, Adrienne, eds., *Critical cyberculture studies*, New York: New York University Press, 2006, chapter 12, pp. 129–139.

Geer, David, "Vendors Upgrade Their Physics Processing to Improve Gaming," *Computer*, August 2006, *vol. 39* (no. 8), pp. 22–24.

Grant, Robert M., *Contemporary Strategy Analysis*, fifth ed., Oxford: Blackwell Publishing, 2005.

Graumann, Sabine and Florian Neinert, "Monitoring Informationswirtschaft - 7. Faktenbericht 2004," Sekundärstudie Nummer 7, TNS Infratest GmbH & Co. KG, München Juni 2004.

Grossmann, Edward, ed., *Game Development – Serious Business, Serious Coding*, Vol. vol. 1 of *ACM Queue - tomorrow's computing today*, New York: ACM, February 2004.

Guadagno, Rosanna and Robert Cialdini, "Online persuasion and complience: social influence on the Internet and beyond," in Yair Amichai-Hamburger, ed., *The Social Net: Understanding human behavior in cyberspace*, Oxford: Oxford University Press, 2005, chapter 4, pp. 91–113.

Hendler, James, "The Dark Side of the Semantic Web," *IEEE Intelligent Systems*, May-June 2007, *vol. 22* (no. 3), pp. 2–4.

Heuskel, Dieter, *Wettbewerb jenseits von Industriegrenzen – Aufbruch zu neuen Wachstumsstrategien*, Frankfurt/Main, New York: Campus Verlag, 1999.

Horsti, Aleksi, Virpi Kristiina Tuunainen, and Jyrki Tolonen, "Evaluation of Electronic Business Model Success: Survey among Leading Finnish Companies," in "Proceedings of the 38th Hawaii International Conference on System Sciences - 2005" IEEE 2005, pp. 189–197.

Hüttl, Tina, "Ohne Kimilu geht's nicht," *Welt am Sonntag*, 11. Februar 2007, *60* (no. 6), p. 67.

IBM, "Emergence of the 3-D Internet," Offering brochure G325-2841-00, IBM Corporation, Somers, NY, USA , April 16th, 2007.

_ , "Virtual Worlds, Real Leaders: Online games put the future of business leadership on display," Global Innovation Outlook 2.0 report, IBM Research, Armonk, NY , June 20th, 2007. (IBM2007c).

James, Daniel, Gordon Walton, Nova Barlow, Elonka Dunin, Edward Castronova, Davis Kennerly, Justin Dolbier, and Justin Quimby, "2004 Persistent Worlds Whitepaper," Whitepaper, IGDA Online Games SIG 2004.

Jüngling, Thomas, "Kapitalismus pur," *Welt am Sonntag*, 11. Februar 2007, *60* (no. 6), p. 66.

Jones, Willie D., "Microsoft and Google Vie for Virtual World Domination," *IEEE Spectrum*, July 2006, *vol. 43* (no. 7), pp. 16–18.

Koenig, M., "Social Networking Means Business in 2007," Market Analysis RA-311, Saugatuck Technology, Westport, CT January 24. 2007.

Koh, Joon, Young-Gul Kim, Brian Butler, and Gee-Woo Bock, "Encouraging Participation in Virtual Communities," *Communications of the ACM*, February 2007, *vol. 50* (no. 2), pp. 69–73.

Kollmann, Tobias, *E-Business - Grundlagen elektronischer Geschäftsprozesse in der Net Economy*, 1. ed., Wiesbaden: Gabler Verlag, Januar 2007.

Kotler, Philip, Veronica Wong, John Saunders, and Gary Armstrong, *Principles of Marketing*, 4th european ed., Harlow, England: Pearson Education, 2005.

Lassila, Ora and James Hendler, "Embracing "Web 3.0"," *IEEE Internet Computing*, May-June 2007, *vol. 11* (no. 3), pp. 90–93.

Lin, Kwei-Jay, "Building Web 2.0," *Computer*, May 2007, *vol. 40* (no. 5), pp. 101–102.

Lindemann, Thomas, "Die Sehnsucht nach dem anderen Leben," *Welt am Sonntag*, 11. Februar 2007, *60* (no. 6), p. 65.

Lober, Andreas, "Auch Second Life kennt Gesetze," *Computer Zeitung*, 7. Mai 2007, *vol. 38* (no. 19), p. 9.

MacInnes, Ian and Lili Hu, "Business Models for Online Communities: The Case of the Virtual Worlds Industry in China," in "Proceedings of the 38th Hawaii International Conference on System Sciences - 2005" IEEE January 2005, pp. 191–200.

Martynow, Jens, *Der Onlinegaming-Markt – Marktüberblick und bestehende Geschäftsmodelle*, Saarbrücken: VDM Verlag Dr. Müller, 2007.

McFedries, Paul, "The Web, Take Two," *IEEE Spectrum*, June 2006, *vol. 43* (no. 6), p. 52.

Narayanan, V.K. and Liam Fahey, "Macroenvironmental Analysis: Understanding the Environment Outside the Industry," in Liam Fahey and Robert M. Randall, eds., *The Portable MBA in Strategy*, second ed., New York: John-Wiley & Sons, Inc., , November 27th, 2000, chapter 9, pp. 189–214.

Nelsetuen, Rodney, "Online Social Worlds as Emerging Markets: A Dose of (Virtual) Reality," ViewPoint issue 165, Tower Group Inc., Needham, MA, USA , July 2006.

Newman, James, *Videogames* Routledge Introductions to Media and Communications, New York: Routledge, 2004.

novomind AG, "Internet World Business Trendscout: Virtuelle Realitäten," Internet survey powerpoint presentation, novomind AG with Internet World Business, Hamburg May 2007.

O'Riordan, Kate, "Gender, Technology, and Visual Cyberculture - Virtually Women," in Silver, David and Massanari, Adrienne, eds., *Critical cyberculture studies*, New York: New York University Press, 2006, chapter 21, pp. 243–254.

Osterwalder, Alexander, Yves Pigneur, and Christopher L. Tucci, "Clarifying Business Models: Origins, Present, and Future of the Concept," *Communications of AIS,* May 2005, *vol. 15.*

Phifer, Gene, Frank Kenney, Yvonne Genovese, David Mitchell Smith, Daniel Sholler, Benoit J. Lheureux, Ray Valdes, Michael James Melenovsky, Cameron Haight, Yefim V. Natis, Michele Cantara, Daryl C. Plummer, Janelle B. Hill, Ray Wagner, Rita E. Knox, Charles Abrams, Whit Andrews, Mark Driver, David W. Cearley, Nikos Drakos, David Gootzit, Andrea Di Maio, James Lundy, Mark R. Gilbert, and Nicholas Gall, "Hype Cycle for Web Technologies, 2006," Research G00141111, Gartner Inc. July 7. 2006.

Point Topic, "World Broadband Statistics Report – Q1 2007," Quarterly statistics report, Point Topic Ltd., London June 2007.

Porter, Michael E., *Competitive Advantage – Creating and Sustaining Superior Performance*, 1. ed., New York: The Free Press, 1985.

__ , *Competitive strategy – techniques for Analyzing Industries and Competitors*, New York: The Free Press, 1998.

Rockart, John F., "Chief Executives Define Their Own Data Needs," *Harvard Business Review*, March-April 1979, *vol. 57* (no. 2), pp. 79–92.

Saunders, Mark, Philip Lewis, and Adrian Thornhill, *Research Methods for Business Students*, second ed., London: Financial Times Prentice Hall, 2007.

Schaap, Frank, "Disaggregation, Technology, and Masculinity: Elements of Internet Research," in Silver, David and Massanari, Adrienne, eds., *Critical cyberculture studies*, New York: New York University Press, 2006, chapter 20, pp. 228–242.

Schneider, Mark C and Sigrun Schubert, "Megatrend Second Life," *Capital*, März 2007, *vol. 46* (no. 06), pp. 18–25.

Scholz, Volker and Marcus A. Magnor, "Texture Replacement of Garments in Monocular Video Sequences," in "Proceedings of the 17th Eurographics Symposium on Rendering (EGSR 2006)" Max-Planck-Institut Nicosia, Cyprus June 2006, pp. 305–312.

Sproull, Lee, Caryn Conley, and Jae Yun Moon, "Prosocial behavior on the net," in Yair Amichai-Hamburger, ed., *The Social Net: Understanding human behavior in cyberspace*, Oxford: Oxford University Press, 2005, chapter 6, pp. 139–161.

Subramanian, Ramkumar, "Demystifying 2.0: Web 2.0, Other Initiatives and the road to NGN2.0," White Paper, Wipro Technologies , March 7th, 2007.

Tan, Margaret, *E-payment – The Digital Exchange*, Singapore: NUS Publishing, 2004.

Tanenbaum, Andrew S., *Computer Networks*, international third ed., London: Prentice Hall International, 1996.

Timmers, Paul H., *Electronic Commerce – Strategies and Models for Business-to-Business Trading* Wiley Series in Information Systems, Chichester: Wiley, 2000.

Vacca, John R., *Virtual Reality: Strategies for Intranet and World Wide Web Applications*, 1st ed., Computer Technology Research Corp., 1996.

Whang, Leo Sang-Min and Geun-Young Chang, "Lifestyles of Virtual World Residents, Living in the on-line game, 'Lineage'," in "Proceedings of the 2003 International Conference on Cyberworlds (CW'03)" IEEE Computer Society 2003, pp. 18–25.

Wirtz, Bernd W., *Electronic Business*, 2. ed., Wiesbaden: Gabler Verlag, Oktober 2001.

Internet resources

ACS Ltd., "Anshe Chung Studios to Link Virtual World Economies," `http://acs.anshechung.com/news_4.php` , Anshe Chung Studios company website, May 21st, 2007. Last access: 29.08.2007, (ACS2007a).

_ , "Facts and Figures," `http://acs.anshechung.com/facts.php` , Anshe Chung Studios company website, 2007. Last access: 29.08.2007.

Activeworlds, "Activeworlds Educational Universe Pricing Information," `http://www.activeworlds.com/edu/awedu_pricing.asp` , Company website, 2007. Last access: 27.07.2007, (Activeworlds2007a).

_ , "Activeworlds Products," `http://www.activeworlds.com/products/index.asp` , Activeworlds company website, 2007. Last access: 27.07.2007.

Blizzard, "10-Day Free Trial," `http://www.worldofwarcraft.com/burningcrusade/trial/index.html?referrer=WORLDOFWARCRAFT&source=wowhome&promo=1` , World of Warcraft product website, 2007. Last access: 25.07.2007, (Blizzard2007a).

Blizzard Press Release, "World of Warcraft surpasses 9 million subscribers worldwide," `http://www.blizzard.com/press/070724.shtml` , Blizzard company website, July 24th, 2007. Last access: 25.07.2007, (Blizzard2007b).

_ , "World of Warcraft: The Burning Crusade™ shatters day-1 sales record," `http://www.blizzard.com/press/070123.shtml` , Blizzard company website, January 23th, 2007. Last access: 25.07.2007.

Bonacker, Volker, "Steuern zahlen für "Second Life"," `http://www2.onspiel e.t-online.de/dyn/c/11/22/32/12/11223212.html` , T-Online Portal: Second Life Special 2007. Last access: 11.07.2007.

Bulkeley, William M., "Playing Well With Others – How IBM's employees have taken social networking to an unusual level," `http://online.wsj.com/public/article_print/SB118194536298737221.html` , The Wall Street Journal Online, June 18th, 2007. Last access: 25.08.2007.

Chai, Winston, "Lawmakers restrict online game in Asia," `http://news.com.com/Lawmakers+restrict+online+game+in+Asia/2100-1043_3-5053209.html` , C-Net News.com, July 23th, 2003. Last access: 11.07.2007.

Chosunilbo, "Landmark Ruling Against *Lineage* Maker Over Data Leak," `http:` `//english.chosun.com/w21data/html/news/200604/20060428002` `6.html` , Digital Chosunilbo (English Edition): Daily News in English About Korea, April 28th, 2006. Last access: 20.07.2007.

Combs, Nate, "RIP: Gaming Open Market?," `http://terranova.blogs.` `com/terra_nova/2005/09/rip_gaming_open.html` , Terra Nova Blog, September 28th, 2005. Last access: 03.08.2007.

Dauser, Thomas and Nick Schader, "YouTube – Fernsehbeitrag von Report Mainz über Kinderpornografie in Second Life," `http://www.youtube.com` `/watch?v=Wk8uNWF77gg` , YouTube video of ARD Report Mainz magazine, May 8th, 2007. Last access: 05.08.2007.

Deep Blue Book, "IBM and Second Life," `http://www.youtube.com/view_` `play_list?p=4A21078F403E9761` , YouTube video playlist of deepbluebook, August 2007. Last access: 29.08.2007.

Dibbell, Julian, "The Life of the Chinese Gold Farmer," `http://www.nytime` `s.com/2007/06/17/magazine/17lootfarmers-t.html?pagewanted` `=1&ei=5090&en=1676d344608cb590&ex=1339732800` , The New York Times Online, June 17th, 2007. Last access: 12.07.2007.

Dickie, Mure, "China moves to zap online game addiction," `http://www.ft.c` `om/cms/s/89ea206a-13f3-11da-af53-00000e2511c8.html` , FT.com (Financial Times), August 23th, 2005. Last access: 11.07.2007.

ESA, "Facts & Research - Game Player Data," `http://www.theesa.com/` `facts/gamer_data.php` , ESA organizational website, 2007. Last access: 07.07.2007.

Friedman, Laurie, "IBM Using Internet's Virtual World to Train Thousands of New Employees in," `http://www.hr.com/servlets/sfs?&t=/Default` `/gateway&i=1116423256281&b=1116423256281&application=stor` `y&active=no&ParentID=1119278002800&StoryID=1163468283729&` `xref=http%3A//www.google.de/search%3Fq%3Dibm+hr+second+li` `fe%26hl%3Den%26client%3Dfirefox-a%26rls%3Dorg.mozilla%3Ae` `n-US%3Aofficial%26hs%3DJSb%26start%3D10%26sa%3DN` , HR.com – The Human Resources Portal , November 14th, 2006. Last access: 25.08.2007.

Heng, Elina, "Entropia Universe enters China to create the largest virtual world ever," `http://www.mindark.com/docs/pr/Entropia_Universe_Ent` `ers_China.pdf` , MindArk PE company website, May 30th, 2007. Last access: 23.08.2007.

Hof, Robert, "A Virtual World's Real Dollars," `http://www.businessweek.` `com/technology/content/mar2006/tc20060328_688225.htm` , Business Week Online, March 28th, 2006. Last access: 31.07.2007.

Hutcheon, Stephen, "Anshe's kinky past revealed," `http://www.smh.com.` `au/articles/2007/01/17/1168709794333.html` , The Sydney Morning Herald Online, January 17th, 2007. Last access: 29.08.2007.

IBM, "Cell Broadband Engine Project Aims to Supercharge IBM Mainframe for Virtual Worlds," `http://www-03.ibm.com/press/us/en/pressre lease/21433.wss` , IBM corporate website – Press room, April 27th, 2007. Last access: 12.07.2007.

_ , "Girls' Day 2007 @ IBM," `http://www-05.ibm.com/employment/de/ life/girlsday.html` , IBM Deutschland corporate website, 2007. Last access: 30.08.2007, (IBM2007e).

_ , "The Greater IBM Connection – Once an IBMer, always a Greater IBMer," `http://www.ibm.com/ibm/greateribm/` , IBM corporate website, 2007. Last access: 25.08.2007, (IBM2007d).

IGE.com, "Our Business," `http://www.ige.com/about` , IGE company website, 2007. Last access: 11.07.2007.

Jacobs, Ian, "Long Description of W3C10 Timeline Graphic," `http://www. w3.org/2005/01/timelines/description` , W3C organizational website, April 2005. Last access: 09.05.2007.

_ , "About W3C - History," `http://www.w3.org/Consortium/history` , W3C organizational website, April 2007. Last access: 09.05.2007.

Jonas, Dow and Walker Spaight, "Did Anshe's Anshe$ Strike Fear in the Wallets of LL?," `http://www.secondlifeherald.com/slh/2006/04/did_ anshes_ansh.html` , The Second Life Herald, April 1st, 2006. Last access: 29.08.2007.

Kutik, Bill, "IBM Brings HR into the Virtual World," `http://www.hreo nline.com/HRE/story.jsp?storyId=9719662` , Human Resource Executive Online, February 12th, 2007. Last access: 25.08.2007.

Linden Research Inc., "Company Fact Sheet," `http://s3.amazonaws.com/ static-secondlife-com/corporate/LindenLab_Facts.pdf` , Linden Lab company website – Press Room, October 24th, 2004. Last access: 31.07. 2007.

_ , "Economic Statistics," `http://www.secondlife.com/whatis/economy _stats.php` , Second Life product website, July 30th, 2007. Last access: 31.07.2007.

_ , "Education," `http://secondlife.com/businesseducation/educat ion.php` , Second Life product website, 2007. Last access: 26.08.2007, (Linden2007b).

_ , "Linden Dollar Exchange," `https://secure-web3.secondlife.com/ currency/index.php` , Second Life product website, 2007. Last access: 03.08.2007, (Linden2007a).

MindArk PE AB, "End User License Agreement," `https://account.entro piauniverse.com/pe/en/rich/5185.html` , Entropia Universe product website, February 6th, 2007. Last access: 31.07.2007, (MindArk2007a).

_ , "Entropia Universe Cash Card," http://www.entropiauniverse.com/en/rich/5676.html , Entropia Universe product website, 2007. Last access: 31.07.2007, (MindArk2007b).

Nelson, Tim D., "CIO Definitions: e-business," http://searchcio.techtarget.com/sDefinition/0,,sid19_gci212026,00.html , CIO Decisions magazine website, July 2001. Last access: 22.05.2007.

O'Reilly, Tim, "What Is Web 2.0: Design Patterns and Business Models for the Next Generation of Software," http://www.oreillynet.com/pub/a/oreilly/tim/news/2005/09/30/what-is-web-20.html , O'Reilly Media company website, September 30th, 2005. Last access: 24.05.2007.

Osterwalder, Alexander, "Business Model Template – designing your competitive edge," http://business-model-design.blogspot.com/2 006/11/business-model-template-designing-your.html , Arvetica company website, November 6th, 2006. Last access: 14.07.2007.

Parlow, Roger, "Virtual Worlds, Real Litigation," http://legalpad.blogs.fortune.com/tag/second-life/ , Fortune magazine – Legal Pad Blog, June 1st, 2007. Last access: 31.07.2007.

Pendragon, Hiro, "Bragg vs. Linden Lab: Bragg Wins Either Way," http://secondtense.blogspot.com/2007/07/bragg-vs-linden-lab-bragg-wins-either.html , Second Tense blogspot, July 15th, 2007. Last access: 31.07.2007.

Rose, Frank, "How Madison Avenue Is Wasting Millions on a Deserted Second Life," http://www.wired.com/techbiz/media/magazine/15-08/ff_sheep?currentPage=all , Wired Magazine Online, July 24th, 2007. Last access: 24.08.2007.

Schoolmann, Gerhard, "Besteuerung von Second Life-Aktivitaeten in Deutschland," http://www.abseits.de/weblog/2007/01/besteuerung-von-second-life.html , Abseits.de blogspot Gastgewerbe Gedankensplitter, January 21st, 2007. Last access: 11.07.2007.

Sony Online Entertainment, "Station Exchange: The Official Secure Marketplace for EverQuest II Players," http://stationexchange.station.sony.com/ , SOE station.com website, 2007. Last access: 02.08.2007.

Thorsen, Tor, "Game-addict clinic opening in Amsterdam," http://www.gamespot.com/news/6152141.html , News at GameSpot.com, June 1st, 2006. Last access: 11.07.2007.

Trantow, Sven, "Second Life – Virtuelle Welt ohne Gesetze," http://www.focus.de/digital/games/second_life/second-life_aid_55693.html , Focus Online, May 8th, 2007. Last access: 20.07.2007.

Wallace, Marc, "Anshe Chung Wins Entropia Banking License," http://www.3pointd.com/20070503/anshe-chung-wins-entropia-banking-license/ , 3pointD.com blogspot, May 3rd, 2007. Last access: 29.08.2007, (Wallace2007a).

_ , "Anshe to Launch Inter-World Financial Market," http://www.3pointd.c om/20070519/anshe-to-launch-inter-world-financial-market/ , 3pointD.com blogspot, May 19th, 2007. Last access: 29.08.2007.

WarcraftRealms.com, "June Concurrency Numbers Calculated," http://www. warcraftrealms.com/ , WarcraftRealms.com website, July 3rd, 2007. Last access: 25.07.2007.

Wikipedia, "Linden Lab," http://en.wikipedia.org/wiki/Linden_Lab , Wikipedia, the free encyclopedia, July 17th, 2007. Last access: 31.07.2007, (Wikipedia2007c).

_ , "Massively multiplayer online game," http://en.wikipedia.org/wi ki/MMO , Wikipedia, the free encyclopedia, August 29th, 2007. Last access: 31.08.2007, (Wikipedia2007e).

_ , "Motion picture rating system," http://en.wikipedia.org/wiki/M otion_picture_rating_system , Wikipedia, the free encyclopedia, July 24th 2007. Last access: 28.07.2007, (Wikipedia2007b).

_ , "StarCraft professional competition," http://en.wikipedia.org/wiki/ StarCraft_professional_competition , Wikipedia, the free encyclope-dia, July 23th, 2007. Last access: 24.07.2007, (Wikipedia2007a).

_ , "World of Warcraft," http://en.wikipedia.org/wiki/WoW , Wikipedia, the free encyclopedia, July 30th, 2007. Last access: 31.07.2007, (Wikipe-dia2007d).

Xing, Wang, "The more they play, the more they lose," http://www.ch inadaily.com.cn/china/2007-04/10/content_846715.htm , China Daily Online, April 10th, 2007. Last access: 11.07.2007.

Zakon, Robert H., "Hobbes' Internet Timeline v8.2," http://www.zakon. org/robert/internet/timeline/ , private website of Robert H. Zakon, November 2006. Last access: 09.05.2007.

www.ingramcontent.com/pod-product-compliance
Lightning Source LLC
Chambersburg PA
CBHW070732220326
41598CB00024BA/3398